Getting It Right
Markets and Choices in a Free Society

Robert J. Barro

The MIT Press
Cambridge, Massachusetts
London, England

Fourth printing, 1998
First MIT Press paperback edition, 1997
© 1996 Massachusetts Institute of Technology

This book was set in Sabon by The MIT Press.
Printed and bound in the United States of America.

Library of Congress Cataloging-in-Publication Data

Barro, Robert J.
  Getting it right : markets and choices in a free society / Robert J. Barro.
    p.   cm.
  Includes index.
  ISBN 0-262-02408-X (H), 0-262-52226-8 (P)
  1. Free enterprise.   2. Libertarianism.   3. Right of property.
4. Democracy.   5. Economic policy.   I. Title
HB95.B365   1996
338.9—dc20   95-26220
                                                          CIP

For Zvi Griliches, my thesis advisor. His willingness to accept
me as a student may have kept me from a life as an accountant.

Contents

Preface

For most of my professional career, I have written technical articles aimed at my fellow economists, and I have prepared textbooks for undergraduate and graduate students. Then in spring 1991, Bob Bartley, the editor of the *Wall Street Journal*, asked me to write articles for the paper's broad audience on a semiregular basis as a contributing editor. Since then I have prepared columns for the *Journal* roughly once every six weeks, and I have also written some pieces for other popular media. This work provided raw material and inspiration for the essays in this book. If people like or dislike this book, then a lot of the credit or blame should go to Bob Bartley.

The preparation of articles for a nontechnical readership has meshed well with my academic research. I think that I have maintained the standards of sound economic reasoning while being forced to explain to noneconomists the implications of this reasoning for a variety of social issues. The only low point came during a panel debate at the American Economic Association meetings in January 1994 when Bob Solow of MIT accused me of behaving like a journalist, a characterization that I was pretty sure was intended as an insult. Probably he was just in a bad mood and was really complaining about my deviations from the New Deal principles that he grew up with.

I did a lot of the work on this book in 1994–1995 while I was Houblon-Norman research fellow at the Bank of England. During that time I benefited especially from interactions with Mervyn King, the Bank's chief economist and executive director, who arranged for my visit. I am also grateful to the Hoover Institution and its director, John Raisian. Many of the ideas in this book were generated during my stays at Hoover.

I developed much of my basic philosophy about economics during my two tenures (1972–1975 and 1982–1984) in the Economics Department of the University of Chicago, especially from interactions with Milton Friedman, George Stigler, Gary Becker, and Bob Lucas. Although it is hard to describe my time spent in Chicago as fun, it must have been healthy medicine.

My longest tenure anywhere (up to this point) was at the University of Rochester (1975–1982, 1984–1987). In contrast to Chicago, Rochester probably treated me better than I deserved. While at Rochester I wrote my first textbook (in macroeconomics) and began an ongoing interaction with Paul Romer on economic growth.

Finally, I am grateful for the congenial, productive atmosphere of the Economics Department of Harvard University. I sometimes feel like the resident right-winger in a liberal establishment, but there is plenty of tolerance and an abundance of intellectual interaction. Anyway, there is a certain scarcity value in representing free-market viewpoints at an institution that is identified with the twentieth century style of liberalism, especially when the institution is the world's most prestigious university.

Introduction

Frankly, I used to be a liberal, in the twentieth-century sense of a left-winger. For any social problem that came up, I had no doubt that the cure involved government intervention, and I could concoct a clever, great society–type program that would fix things. I also had the usual liberal view that most conservatives were stupid or greedy.

This attitude remained firm until I was nineteen or twenty and a college student at Caltech. I have a hard time pinpointing the knowledge and experience that started my transformation into a libertarian or, perhaps more precisely, a classical liberal. Certainly the exposure to economics—a little at Caltech and more in the Ph.D. program at Harvard—helped. Yet this material was mostly interventionist when it had a policy slant—not at all the free-market perspective of the Chicago school. Many of my left-wing colleagues learned the same economics and still retained the left-wing political views that I had when I was sixteen. (I find to this day that the similarity of many left-wing arguments to my teenage opinions helps me as a debater. I can understand the beliefs—and misconceptions—of liberals in a way that would be impossible if I had never suffered from the same disease.)

One turning point came in 1964 when John Kenneth Galbraith gave a speech at Caltech in support of Lyndon

Johnson's campaign for the presidency. At the time, Galbraith was one of my heroes, and I awaited his speech eagerly. But I recall a keen sense of disappointment with my recognition that his commentary on economics and society made little sense. In 1964, I attributed the shortcomings to his having a bad day; I learned later that the problem was more systematic.

Much of the Ph.D. program at Harvard was technical economics and essentially apolitical. There was the occasional ridicule of Milton Friedman, partly in the context of his monetary theory and partly on his views on free markets and the proper, limited role of government. Even before I left Harvard in the summer of 1968, I recognized that the attacks on Milton were empty and mainly a sign of envy. But I still must have been a liberal, because I voted for Bobby Kennedy (by absentee ballot) in the ill-fated 1968 California primary.

Also helpful to my transformation in a negative way was the experience of my first job, as assistant professor at Brown University. Brown between 1968 and 1971 was a remarkably left-wing place, with the administration caving in to radical protests at every opportunity. Somehow the Vietnam War was taken as a legitimate excuse for destroying a system of quality education that had been developed over many decades. The faculty even endorsed a new curriculum that abolished grades and embraced an array of touchy-feely courses on unorthodox subjects. This program was devised by a genius undergraduate, Ira Magaziner, who was later to contribute his alleged talents to the recently failed reform effort of the U.S. health care system.

Overall, I rejected liberalism by the early 1970s, before I had a fully articulated philosophy as a replacement. But I was already moving toward a free-market outlook, and this transition was aided by my tenure on the faculty of the economics department of the University of Chicago from 1972 to 1975.

(Many people infer incorrectly from my writings that I must have been a student in Chicago.) Aside from Milton Friedman, I was heavily influenced by Gary Becker and George Stigler. (Gary was pleased that a reviewer of this book described many of my ideas as Beckeresque.) I particularly learned a lot in Chicago about the role of markets, the applicability of economic reasoning to a wide range of social issues, and the interplay between economics and politics.

I would describe my philosophy—the one that I have adopted and shaped since the early 1970s and that guides this book—as libertarian (or classical liberal), rather than conservative or Republican. (Nevertheless, I loved the opinion of one reviewer that I was "a conservative who takes no prisoners.") My view is not anarchic; I believe that government has some key functions, notably to define and protect property rights. This heading encompasses national and domestic security and the enactment and enforcement of a system of laws and contracts. Other important governmental activities include ensuring (but not producing) a baseline level of education, providing a minimal welfare net, and participating in a narrow range of infrastructure investments, such as highways and airports. My belief in the appropriateness of this limited range of public functions is consistent with the view that most governments have gone much too far in their expenditures, taxation, and regulations.

My perspective is not conservative in the sense of maintenance of the status quo, because I favor an activist approach that would eliminate many of the government's existing programs. My view is also not conservative in the modern social sense. I differ, for example, with many proposals offered by the Pat Buchanan wing of the Republican party: such nonlibertarian acts as heavy restrictions on abortion rights, promotion of prayer in public schools, enforcement of strict drug laws, curbs on immigration, and restraints on international trade.

My views are more akin to the nineteenth-century liberal philosophy espoused by Milton Friedman, especially in his *Capitalism and Freedom*. In that work, he proposed many policies that are harmonious with free markets and are receiving serious attention in the United States and other countries. This list includes school choice, the flat-rate income tax, rules for monetary stability, privatized social security, and the elimination of affirmative-action programs. (On the other hand, I regard Milton's macroeconomics as far too Keynesian.)

A dominant theme throughout this book is the importance of institutions that ensure property rights and free markets. The discussion deals especially with the appropriate range of functions of government—which areas represent useful public policy and which unnecessary interference.

The first section considers these questions in the context of the determinants of long-run economic growth. In addition to the basic economic forces, I assess related political topics, such as the role of democratic institutions, the optimal size of countries, and the consequences of default on sovereign debt.

The second section deals with the proper role and form of monetary policy. I argue that the government should provide private markets with a stable nominal framework and then mainly stay out of the way. These ideas fit with my general approach to property rights and free markets; that is, price stability emerges from the application of these principles to the monetary area. (Some observers may say that I have not gone far enough by failing to advocate the government's departure from currency issue.)

The third section covers fiscal and other macroeconomic policies. I consider such topics as the distorting influences of taxation, the impact of infrastructure investment and other types of government spending, and the consequences of public debt and budget deficits. These issues relate to economic efficiency—for example, to the incentives for investment and growth—and also to inequality and the rule of law.

Finally, I go beyond macroeconomic issues—the primary area of my professional work—to apply the basic themes to a number of microeconomic subjects: cartels, tax amnesties, school choice programs, privatization, regulation of cigarette smoking, protection of endangered species, the market for baseball players, and the effects of term limits for politicians. Readers will recognize in these applications a consistent approach to markets, institutions, and government.

I have sometimes been criticized for being too predictable. But what would it mean to be unpredictable? That one lacks a coherent framework that can deliver logical answers to well-posed questions? That one gets a different answer to essentially the same question the second time it is asked?

The way that a model applies to a particular subject may sometimes be subtle, and, thus, the range of applicability of the approach may be surprising. But once the application is made, the results ought usually to follow in a straightforward, predictable manner. Therefore, I hope that readers will not be surprised too often by the analysis in this book but will nevertheless be stimulated by the breadth of topics that can be addressed by the consistent application of a few basic principles.

1

Economic Growth

Democracy and Growth

It sounds nice to try to install democracy in places like Haiti and Somalia, but does it make any sense? Would an increase in political freedom tend to spur economic freedoms—specifically property rights and free markets—and thereby spur economic growth? Is there a reasonable prospect that democratic institutions can be maintained in places with such low standards of living? History provides reasonably clear, even if unpleasant, answers to these questions. More political rights do not have an important impact on growth, but improvements in a broad concept of the standard of living tend strongly to precede expansions of political freedoms. In particular, democracies that arise in poor countries—sometimes because they are imposed from outside—typically do not last.

Theoretically, the effect of more democracy on growth is ambiguous. Some observers, such as Milton Friedman in *Capitalism and Freedom*, argue that political and economic freedoms are mutually reinforcing. In this view, an expansion of political rights—more "democracy"—fosters economic rights and tends thereby to stimulate growth.

But the growth-retarding features of democracy have also been stressed. One such mechanism is the tendency of majority voting to support social programs that redistribute income from rich to poor. These programs include graduated-rate income tax systems, land reforms, and welfare transfers. These activities may be desirable in some circumstances, but the required increases in marginal tax rates and other distortions inevitably reduce the incentives for investment, work effort, and growth.

Another adverse feature of representative democracy is the strong political power of interest groups, such as agriculture, environmental lobbies, defense contractors, and the handicapped. These groups tend to generate policies that redistribute resources in favor of themselves. These transfers create economic distortions that hamper growth, and the programs usually do not benefit the poor.

Authoritarian regimes may partially avoid these drawbacks of democracy. Moreover, nothing in principle prevents nondemocratic governments from maintaining economic freedoms and private property. A dictator does not have to engage in central planning. Recent examples of autocracies that have expanded economic freedoms include the Pinochet government in Chile, the Fujimori administration in Peru, to a lesser extent the shah's government in Iran, and several previous and current regimes in East Asia. Furthermore, most OECD (Organization of Economic Cooperation and Development) countries began their modern economic development in systems with limited political rights and became full-fledged representative democracies only much later.

The effects of autocracy on growth are adverse, however, if a dictator uses his or her power to steal the nation's wealth and carry out nonproductive investments. Many governments in

Africa, some in Latin America, some in the formerly planned economies of Eastern Europe, and the Marcos administration in the Philippines seem to fit this model.

Thus, history suggests that dictators come in two types: one whose personal objectives often conflict with growth promotion and another whose interests dictate a preoccupation with economic development. The theory that determines which kind of dictatorship will prevail is missing. Absent this theory, the choice of a dictatorship can be viewed as a risky investment: economic outcomes may be very good or very bad but are surely uncertain.

Democratic institutions may avoid the worst types of results because they provide a check on governmental power. In particular, this check limits the potential of public officials to amass personal wealth and to carry out unpopular policies. Since at least some policies that stimulate growth will also be politically popular, more political rights tend to be growth enhancing on this count.

Overall, there is an abundance of interesting theories that relate democracy to growth, but these theories differ as to whether more democracy is favorable or unfavorable for growth. The net relation is therefore theoretically inconclusive, and we shall have to rely on empirical evidence to sort out the net effect.

The impact of democracy on growth is one thing; the other channel of influence is from economic development to a country's propensity to experience democracy. This issue requires a positive analysis of the choice of political institutions, but theoretical models of this process are not well developed. Nevertheless, a common view—put forward by Seymour Martin Lipset in an article in 1959 (and attributed by him to Aristotle)—is that prosperity tends to inspire democracy. Although this "Lipset hypothesis" lacks a fully articulated theoretical foundation, it has been supported by many case studies.

It is possible to quantify and test the various hypotheses about the interaction between democracy and economic growth. Statistical analysis of data for around a hundred countries from 1960 to 1990 reveals a number of variables that systematically influence the growth rate of real per capita gross domestic product (GDP). The growth rate tends to be higher if a country has more human capital in the forms of health and education, a lower fertility rate, and less government spending on consumption. Also helpful are smaller distortions of market prices and an inclination and ability of the government to protect property rights. (The empirical measure of this last variable comes from a subjective index of the degree to which governments maintain the rule of law. These data, prepared for international investors by a consulting firm, were assembled in a study at American University by Stephen Knack and Philip Keefer, "Institutions and Economic Performance: Cross-Country Tests Using Alternative Institutional Measures.") An improvement in the terms of trade has a small positive effect on growth, and a high propensity to invest also looks moderately favorable.

For given values of the variables already mentioned, the growth rate tends to be higher if a country starts with a lower level of real per capita GDP. That is, if a poor country can maintain satisfactory government policies and accumulate a reasonable level of human capital, then it tends to converge toward the richer places. Examples of this process are the high growth rates from 1960 to 1990 of some East Asian countries: Hong Kong, Singapore, South Korea, Taiwan, Malaysia, Indonesia, and Thailand. However, one reason that most poor countries remain poor is that their governments distort markets to a high degree and fail to maintain property rights.

A key question is the effect of democracy on growth for given values of the other variables. To address this issue I mea-

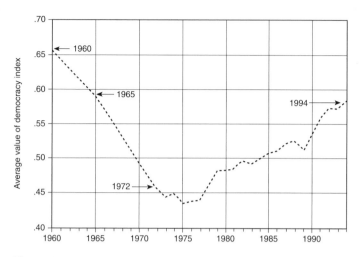

Figure 1
Democracy in the world, 1960–1994. Source: Barro 1996.

sured the degree of democracy by the indicator of political rights compiled for nearly all countries by Raymond Gastil and his followers in the serial publication *Freedom in the World.* The Gastil concept of political rights is indicated by his basic definition: "Political rights are rights to participate meaningfully in the political process. In a democracy this means the right of all adults to vote and compete for public office, and for elected representatives to have a decisive vote on public policies" (Gastil, 1986–1987 edition, p. 7). Thus, the definition is a relatively narrow one, which focuses on the role of elections and elected representatives.

Figure 1 shows the time path of the unweighted average of the democracy index for the available dates: 1960, 1965, and 1972–1994. (The values for 1960 and 1965 come from an article by Kenneth Bollen in the 1990 issue of *Studies in Comparative International Development.*) The index has been expressed here on a scale from zero to one, with zero indicating essentially no rights and one signifying the fullest rights. The number of countries covered rose from 98 in 1960, to 109 in 1965, and 134 from 1972 to 1994. The figure shows that the average value of the democracy index peaked at 0.66 in 1960, fell to a low point of 0.44 in 1975, and rose subsequently to 0.58 in 1994. An important element behind this pattern is the experience in sub-Saharan Africa. Many of these countries began with democratic institutions when they became independent in the early 1960s, but most had evolved into nondemocratic states by the early 1970s. More recently, the extent of democracy in Africa and elsewhere has increased somewhat.

The net effect of more political freedom on growth is theoretically ambiguous. The quantitative analysis indicates that the overall effect is weakly negative but not statistically different from zero. There is some indication of a nonlinear relation in which more democracy raises growth when political freedoms are weak but depresses growth when a moderate amount of freedom has already been attained.

A story behind this relationship is that limitations on the ruler's power are the critical concern for an absolute dictatorship; hence, in this region, more democracy is positive for growth. When political freedom rises above a certain level—corresponding roughly in the empirical analysis to the situation of Mexico or Taiwan in 1994—then further expansions of democracy create great pressure for social programs that redistribute wealth. These programs dilute incentives for investment and work effort and are therefore adverse for growth.

Democracy may also influence growth indirectly by affecting some of the variables that the statistical analysis holds constant. For example, democracy might stimulate female education (by promoting equality among the sexes), which in turn reduces fertility and infant mortality and thereby promotes growth. However, if fertility and female schooling are not held constant, then the overall effect of democracy on growth is still negative.

Another possibility is that democracy encourages maintenance of the rule of law. Although tests of this hypothesis are hampered by the limited availability of data on the rule-of-law concept, the information available suggests that, if anything, democracy is a moderate deterrent to the maintenance of the rule of law. This result is not surprising because more democracy means that the political process allows the majority to extract resources legally from minorities (or powerful interest groups to extract resources legally from the disorganized majority).

Good theories of why democracy expands or contracts seem to be missing. A look at the data suggests, however, that countries at low levels of development typically do not sustain democracy. For example, the political freedoms installed in most of the newly independent African states in the early 1960s did not last. Conversely, nondemocratic places that experience substantial economic development have a tendency to become more democratic—for example, Chile, Peru, Korea, Taiwan, Spain, and Portugal.

Formal statistical analysis demonstrates that countries with higher standards of living—measured by real per capita GDP, infant mortality, and male and female schooling—tend to approach higher levels of democracy over time. For example, a nondemocratic place with a high standard of living is predicted to become more democratic in the future. Conversely, a democratic country with a low standard of living is expected to lose political rights over time.

The results can be used to forecast changes in the level of democracy from the last value observed, 1994, into the future.

Table 1
Countries forecasted to experience major changes in democracy

Projected to be more democratic

Country	Democracy 1994	Democracy 2000
Indonesia	0.00	0.43
Bahrain	0.17	0.52
Hong Kong	0.33	0.67
Algeria	0.00	0.33
Syria	0.00	0.32
Singapore	0.33	0.61
Iran	0.17	0.41
Yugoslavia	0.17	0.41
Sudan	0.00	0.24
Gambia	0.00	0.24
Mexico	0.50	0.72
Tunisia	0.17	0.38
Iraq	0.00	0.21
Swaziland	0.17	0.35
Fiji	0.50	0.69
Sri Lanka	0.50	0.67
Peru	0.33	0.51
Turkey	0.33	0.50
Dominican Republic	0.50	0.66
Japan	0.83	0.98

Source: Barro 1996.

Table 1 displays the cases of especially large projected changes in democracy from 1994 to 2000. The group with large anticipated increases, on the left side of the table, includes some countries that had virtually no political freedom in 1994. Some of these are among the world's poorest countries, such as Sudan and Gambia, for which the projected level of democracy in 2000 is also not high. These countries are forecasted to raise their levels

Table 1
(continued)

Projected to be less democratic

Country	Democracy 1994	Democracy 2000
Malawi	0.83	0.33
Mali	0.83	0.44
Benin	0.83	0.51
Zambia	0.67	0.35
Guinea-Bissau	0.67	0.35
Mozambique	0.67	0.36
Central African Republic	0.67	0.37
Niger	0.67	0.38
Bangladesh	0.83	0.56
Bolivia	0.83	0.58
Hungary	1.00	0.81
Pakistan	0.67	0.48
Mauritius	1.00	0.81
Papua New Guinea	0.83	0.65
South Africa	0.83	0.66
Botswana	0.83	0.66
Congo	0.50	0.36

Note: The democracy index in 1994 is the value derived from the categories of political rights presented in *Freedom in the World*. The value in 2000 is the projection based on the statistical analysis discussed in the text.

of democracy from 0 in 1994 to 0.24 in 2000, that is, roughly one-quarter of the way toward a full representative democracy. (Gambia is interesting in that it had maintained democracy for many years before a coup occurred in July 1994.)

Some other countries that had essentially no political freedom in 1994 are more well off economically and are therefore forecast to have greater increases in democracy; for example, the projected value in 2000 is 0.43 for Indonesia, 0.33 for Algeria, and 0.32 for Syria.

Expectations for large increases in democracy also apply to some reasonably prosperous places in which some political freedoms exist, but to an extent that lags behind the standard of living. As examples, Singapore is projected to increase its democracy index from 0.33 in 1994 to 0.61 in 2000, and Mexico is expected to go from 0.50 to 0.72.

The cases of large expected decreases in democracy, shown on the right side of table 1, consist mainly of relatively poor countries with surprisingly high levels of political freedom in 1994. Many of these are African countries in which the political institutions recently became more democratic: Malawi, Mali, Benin, Zambia, Guinea-Bissau, Mozambique, Central African Republic, and Niger. The prediction, as with the African experience of the 1960s, is that democracy that gets well ahead of economic development will not last. Two other African countries, Mauritius (which is not actually African) and Botswana, have maintained democratic institutions for some time, but the analysis still predicts that political freedoms will diminish in these places.

South Africa is also included on the right side of the table, with a projected decrease in the democracy index from 0.83 in 1994 to 0.66 in 2000. The political changes in South Africa raised the democracy indicator from 0.33 in 1993 to 0.83 in 1994. The statistical analysis says that this change was in the predicted direction but has likely overshot the long-run level.

To summarize, the interplay between democracy and economic development involves the effect of political freedom on growth and the influence of the standard of living on the extent of democracy. With respect to the determination of growth, the cross-country analysis brings out favorable effects from maintenance of the rule of law, free markets, small government consumption, and high human capital. Once these kinds of variables are held constant, an increase in political freedom has an overall negative (but small) impact on growth. The effect is positive at low levels of democracy but negative at higher levels.

With respect to the impact of economic development on democracy, the analysis shows that improvements in the standard of living—measured by a country's real per capita GDP, infant mortality, and education—substantially raise the probability that political institutions will become more democratic over time. Hence, political freedom emerges as a sort of luxury good. Rich places consume more democracy because this good is desirable for its own sake and even though the increased political freedom may have a small adverse effect on growth. Basically, rich countries can afford the reduced rate of economic progress.

The analysis has implications for the desirability of exporting democratic institutions from the advanced Western countries to developing nations. The first lesson is that more democracy is not the key to economic growth, although it may have a small beneficial effect for countries that start with few political rights. The second message is that political freedoms tend to erode over time if they get out of line with a country's standard of living.

The more general conclusion is that the advanced Western countries would contribute more to the welfare of poor nations by exporting their economic systems, notably property rights and free markets, rather than their political systems, which typically developed after reasonable standards of living had been attained. If economic freedom can be established in a poor country, then growth would be encouraged, and the country would tend eventually to become more democratic on its own. Thus, in the long run, the propagation of Western-style economic systems would also be the effective way to expand democracy in the world.

Eastern Germany and the Iron Law of Convergence

How fast will the poor regions of east Germany catch up to the prosperous west? Some optimistic forecasts made at the time of unification in 1990 focused on a projected dramatic response of enterprise to a lifting of repression, but this optimism was tempered by declines in output and increases in unemployment in the east. Real GDP per person fell by about 18 percent from 1990 to 1991 but has since grown rapidly—at about 8 percent per year—to surpass the 1990 level in 1994. What are the long-term prospects?

In postunification Germany, the eastern provinces amount to backward regions of a country that has a single central government, language, and so on. The history of the industrialized countries provides a lot of information about convergence between poor and rich regions. We can look, for example, at the experience of the U.S. South in the century plus after the Civil War, at the economic development of southern Italy since World War II, and at the recent growth performance of Schleswig-Holstein, the poorest area of the former West Germany. Although the transitional problems for the eastern regions of Germany are not the same as those of any of these cases taken individually, we can get useful information from the average experience of many poor regions at various times.

Figure 2 shows the behavior of real per capita personal income from 1880 to 1990 for the four U.S. regions: East, South, Midwest, and West. The good news is that the poor regions tended to grow significantly faster in per capita terms than the rich regions; hence, the wide dispersion in incomes

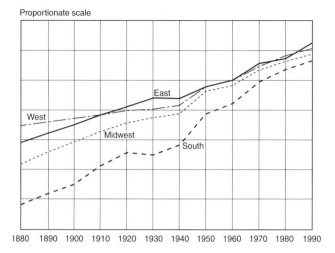

Proportionate scale

1880 1890 1900 1910 1920 1930 1940 1950 1960 1970 1980 1990

Figure 2
Personal income of U.S. regions, 1880–1990. Source: Barro and Sala-i-Martin 1991.

shown in 1880 had essentially disappeared by the 1980s. This process involves the catch-up of the southern states (which became notably poor only with the Civil War) and the slow per capita growth of some western states (which had high per capita incomes in 1880 because of temporary opportunities in mining).

Convergence occurs also within regions. For example, the relatively poor eastern states (such as Maine and Vermont in 1880) tended to catch up to the relatively rich eastern states (Massachusetts and Rhode Island in 1880) about as fast as the typically poor southern states tended to catch up to the typically better off western or eastern states. The convergence process applies to recent periods as well as to the long history; for example, the southern states did especially well in terms of per capita growth from 1940 to 1970.

The bad news from the U.S. experience is that, first, the tendency toward convergence can sometimes be overwhelmed by economic or political events (such as shocks to agriculture or oil or the effects from wartime) and, second, convergence usually takes a long time. On average, about 2 percent of the gap between a poor and rich state vanishes in a year. This numerical estimate, which tends to show up also for countries, has been dubbed the "iron law of convergence" by Larry Summers, my former colleague at Harvard University. This slow pace of adjustment means that the "half-life"—the expected time that it takes to eliminate half of the initial spread—is about thirty-five years.

There were substantial spreads in estimates of East German productivity just before unification in 1990; a reasonable range is from one-third to one-half the West German value. An extrapolation of the U.S. experience to the eastern regions of unified Germany implies that per capita growth in the east would be initially 1 1/2 to 2 percentage points per year higher than in the west. This growth advantage (which is predicted to decline over time as the east converges to the west) means that it takes about fourteen years to eliminate one-quarter of the initial productivity gap, about thirty-five years to eliminate one-half of the gap, and almost seventy years to eliminate three-quarters of the gap. Thus, the east would eventually get close to the west, but the process will likely take a couple of generations rather than a couple of years or even decades.

Better lessons for unified Germany may come from the history of regional growth in Western Europe, including West Germany. The convergence observed for the United States applies also to ninety regions of eight European countries (Belgium, Denmark, France, Italy, the Netherlands, Spain, the United Kingdom, and West Germany). Regions with lower per capita GDP in 1950 tended to grow faster in per capita terms from 1950 to 1990. But as for the United States, the convergence process is slow: the gap between poor and rich tends again to disappear at only the iron-law rate of around 2 percent per year. Thus, an extrapolation of the behavior from the regions of Western Europe leads to the same predictions for the east of Germany that derived from the U.S. experience.

One part of the European story is the famous spread between the north and south of Italy. In 1950, the per capita GDP of four prosperous northern regions was 70 percent above the mean for Italy, whereas the per capita GDP of seven poor southern regions was 32 percent below the mean. In contrast, in 1990, the four northern regions were 30 percent above the mean, and the seven southern regions were 26 percent below the mean. Although the north-south gap remained large in 1990—thus encouraging the popular view that the backward regions in the south would never catch up to the advanced regions in the north—the extent of the reduction of the gap over forty years was, in fact, reasonably in line with the usual relationship. The south of Italy had not caught up to the north by 1990 because it started far away in 1950, and the normal rate of catch-up is not very fast.

Perhaps most relevant for eastern Germany is the experience of the four regions of West Germany that had the lowest per capita GDP in 1950: Schleswig-Holstein, Lower Saxony, Rhineland-Palatinate, and Bavaria. The per capita GDP of these four regions went from 23 percent below the West German average in 1950 to 13 percent below in 1990. Again, the rate of convergence accords with the usual, slow adjustment process.

Regional differences in per capita incomes encourage migration from poor to rich places. The history of the U.S. states provides a basis for predicting the extent of the migration from the east of Germany to the west. The extrapolation of the U.S. results implies that the net migration of persons from the east of Germany to the west would be about 200,000 in 1991 (1.2 percent of the east's population) if the east's productivity in 1990 were one-half the west's and about 340,000 (2.1 percent of the population) if the east's productivity were one-third of the west's. The actual flow of 250,000 fell within this range of estimates.

The projected flow of migrants declines over time for two reasons. First, the convergence process implies that the east's per capita income rises (slowly) relative to the west's, and second, the cumulated migration implies that the west's population density rises relative to the east's (and thereby makes the west relatively less attractive). The combination of these two forces implies that the predicted annual number of net migrants falls to a range of 140,000 to 230,000 by the year 2001; the projected cumulative number of migrants for 1991–2001 is 1.7 to 2.8 million. (The numbers observed through 1994 accord reasonably well with these projections; the number was 199,000 for 1992, 172,000 for 1993, and 73,000 for the first half of 1994.)

The bottom line is that the levels of per capita product and income in the east of Germany can be expected to catch up to the levels in the west, but only at a slow pace that extends over a couple of generations. During the long transition, the average per capita growth rate in the east will exceed that in the west— initially by 1 1/2 to 2 percentage points per year—but the relative performance over short intervals can be better or worse than the projected amount because of a variety of economic and political factors. The transition will also feature large migrations of persons from the east of Germany to the west.

No doubt, the slowness of the adjustment and the substantial movement of persons will create pressures for the German government to speed up the process. The government has, in fact, provided massive subsidies to investment and employment in the east and has also given large-scale transfer payments. The history of regional growth for the United States and Western Europe does not suggest, however, that the government can substantially accelerate the process of convergence in the long run. The forces of convergence are powerful eventually, but anything approaching parity between the east and the west of Germany is unimaginable in the short run.

Epilogue

Recently available data from the Statistiches Bundesamt indicate that in 1990 the real per capita GDP in the western parts of Germany was 2.5 times that in the east. In 1991, the fall in the eastern per capita GDP by 18 percent raised the ratio to 3.2. From 1991 to 1994, the real per capita GDP in the east grew at 8.0 percent per year, compared with –0.1 percent per year in the west. The corresponding ratio of west to east per capita GDP in 1994 was 2.5, the same as that in 1990.

These figures mean that the convergence process—the rate at which the gap between west and east is being closed—is nil if the starting point is 1990 but very strong—around 8 percent per year—if the starting point is 1991. The surprisingly fast rate of convergence since 1991 must reflect in part the German government's subsidies to economic activity in the east. (The low rate of productivity growth in the west likely reflects the high tax rates required to finance this generosity.) Thus, one source of uncertainty for projections is whether these subsidies will be continued or expanded. Overall, there is not yet enough information in 1995 to tell whether Germany will be able to beat the iron-law rate of convergence in the long run.

New and Old Theories of Economic Growth

Background

In the academic literature, the theory of growth that reached its zenith in the 1960s is called neoclassical; the more recent vintage that began in the mid-1980s is called endogenous. In the neoclassical model, a key element is that diminishing returns to capital imply that an economy's per capita growth rate shrinks in the long run to a value determined exogenously (from outside the model) by technological progress. (The growth rate of the level of output depends in addition on population growth, which is also taken as exogenous in the standard framework.) In contrast, the newer models determine technological progress—and, hence, the long-term per capita growth rate—endogenously (within the model). Thus, in the neoclassical model, shifts in the willingness to save or in government policies cannot affect an economy's long-run per capita growth rate. In endogenous growth models, shifts in saving propensities and government policies may have important effects on growth in the long run.

Remarkably, these academic issues became a hot political issue in the United Kingdom in the fall of 1994 when the shadow chancellor of the exchequer for the Labour party, Gordon Brown, noted that the new endogenous growth theory was a key theoretical advance. He argued, moreover, that this theory supported governmental interventions into the economy, not only along the lines of education and infrastructure investment but also extending to industrial policies and labor market regulations. Thus, the new theories apparently supported many policies that the Labour party had always endorsed!

The chancellor, Kenneth Clarke of the Conservative party, responded mainly with jokes, suggesting that *endogenous* and *neoclassical* were funny terms to be introduced into the political fray (and he frequently replaced *endogenous* with *indigenous*—perhaps inadvertently perhaps not). This anti-intellectual response was unfortunate; in response, the *Financial Times* asked me to prepare an article (on which the following commentary is based) to clarify the issues surrounding the various theories of economic growth.

I learned later that the suggestion for this article originated with Gordon Brown's economic adviser, Ed Balls, who previously received training in economics at the Kennedy School of Harvard University. Although Mr. Balls knew that I would disagree with Mr. Brown's policy inferences, he also felt that an intellectual treatment of the subject would benefit the Labour party at the expense of the Conservatives and their anti-intellectual approach.

The Essay

It is hard to know which discussion of growth theories to prefer. The shadow chancellor, Gordon Brown, seems serious in his attempts to understand and apply the ideas, but he ends up with a confused effort to rationalize government intervention into the economy. Then the chancellor, Kenneth Clarke, dwells on the funny sound of endogenous growth and depicts it as some sort of econo-babble that he need not try to understand. I suppose if it really were "indigenous growth," as he described it, then he would be correct.

With some temerity, I venture to explain the origins of endogenous growth and its relation to the older neoclassical theory. The neoclassical model, developed in the 1950s and 1960s, assumed diminishing returns to capital, whether machines and buildings or education of persons. The growth of per capita income could therefore not be sustained in the long run unless the economy broke out of these diminishing returns by introducing new technologies. The rate of technological progress was, however, treated as exogenous in the standard model—not as a matter of principle but because the necessary theoretical advances had not yet been made. As a consequence, the economy's long-run growth rate was exogenous, not driven by elements that were explained within the theory.

This result does not mean that investment and government policy play no role in the neoclassical model. More investment and better policy (lower marginal tax rates, more productive infrastructure, better enforcements of laws and contracts, price stability) increase growth for a long time, even if not forever. It is only in the very long run that growth is exogenous in the neoclassical framework.

In the late 1980s, Paul Romer (then a Ph.D. student in Chicago and now a professor at the University of California, Berkeley) worked out a theory in which commercial research and development led to the discovery and adoption of new technologies, products, and ideas. The rate of technological advance and, hence, the economy's long-run growth rate then became endogenous in the sense that they were explained within the model. A crucial element in this theory (reminiscent of ideas expressed sixty years earlier by the famous economist Joseph Schumpeter) is the reward given to innovators; in the absence of such a prize, would-be entrepreneurs have no incentive to carry out costly and often unsuccessful research projects. Typically, the reward takes the form of a temporary period of monopoly power during which a new product or the fruits of an improved technology are priced above the competitive level.

In Romer's model, the growth rate need not be socially optimal; that is, Adam Smith's invisible hand need not work perfectly. Many observers have taken this result as a license to advocate their favorite forms of government intervention, whether trade restrictions, subsidies or protection for favored industries, labor market regulations, and so on. In fact, the main policy implications from the model are a rationale for public support of basic research and a more favorable view of monopoly in high-growth sectors. Many standard kinds of interventions—such as industrial policies aimed at picking technological winners, distortions of international trade, and restrictions of labor markets—tend to be more adverse than usual because they affect long-term growth rates, not just static allocations of resources. There is no reasonable way to use endogenous growth theory to rationalize policies such as minimum wage rates, strong labor unions, housing subsidies, and large transfer payments.

From an empirical standpoint, the most successful framework has proved to be a combination of the new, endogenous growth theory with the older, neoclassical model. The new theory explains the growth performance of technological leaders, in particular, why these countries—and therefore the world as a whole—can grow for centuries without tending to slow down. The older model explains why and when the lagging countries tend to converge toward the leaders.

Statistical analysis of data for around a hundred countries from 1960 to 1990 reveals a number of variables that systematically influence the growth rate of real per capita GDP. The growth rate tends to be higher if the government protects property rights, maintains free markets, and spends little on nonproductive consumption. Also helpful are high levels of human capital in the forms of education and health, low fertility rates, and improvements in the terms of trade with other countries. More public investment in transport and communications (forms of infrastructure) may be useful, but the present evidence does not reveal supernormal rates of return in these areas. High investment in general looks only moderately favorable because this investment seems mainly to be a response to the underlying environment and the prospects for growth.

For given values of the variables already mentioned, the growth rate tends to be higher if a country starts with a lower level of real per capita GDP. That is, if a poor country can maintain good government policies and accumulate a reasonable level of human capital, then it tends to converge toward the richer places. (This force seems to underlie the East Asian success stories.) However, one reason that most poor countries remain poor is that their governments distort markets and fail to protect property rights.

Overall, the recent theory and empirical work on economic growth supports the general thrust of the economic policies undertaken in the United Kingdom by the Conservative party since Margaret Thatcher's ascension to power in 1979. Thus, it is surprising that Chancellor Clarke chose to ridicule this recent research with anti-intellectual jokes. I suppose that I will never understand British humor.

A Tale of Two Cities (Growth in Hong Kong and Singapore)

The city-states of Hong Kong and Singapore are two of the heroes of economic development. Gross domestic product per capita grew in both countries at a remarkable 6 percent per year from 1960 to 1990, and the levels of per capita product advanced in each country from one-quarter of the U.S. level in 1960 to about three-quarters in 1990. These success stories motivate a look at the detailed histories to find clues about the policies that contribute to growth. The investigation is especially revealing because the governmental actions pursued by Hong Kong and Singapore have been polar opposites in major ways. Hong Kong has been largely laissez faire, whereas Singapore has pursued an aggressive form of industrial policy.

We should begin with some of the many similarities of the two countries: small city-states that began under British colonialism as trading centers with immigrant populations from China. Neither country has significant agriculture or natural resources, except for harbors. Both economies are highly open to international trade and have high ratios of exports and imports to GDP. Neither government imposes much direct regulations on business, and neither has high ratios of government consumption purchases or transfer payments to GDP. Each has been politically stable for some time, although Singapore had difficulties in the 1960s, and Hong Kong's prospects after the reinstatement of Chinese rule in 1997 are uncertain. The two countries are nearly identical in age-adjusted fertility and mortality rates, although Hong Kong had somewhat higher population growth due to greater in-migration. Hong Kong's population had significantly more educational attainment in 1960 and continues to enjoy an educational advantage today.

The list of differences could start with Singapore's constraints on civil liberties, illustrated by its limitations on the circulation of the *Wall Street Journal* (a constraint that no doubt limited the Singaporeans' access to the latest innovations in economic thought). More important contrasts from an economic standpoint involve the government's role in three areas: the volume of saving and investment, the role of foreign investment, and the amount of spending on public infrastructure. Singapore has been far more activist in these areas, especially in using the tax and pension systems to compel private saving and to subsidize foreign investment and entrepreneurship in targeted industries. Its direct public investment has also been much greater than Hong Kong's. Hong Kong has, in general, been far less interventionist. The major exception is its monopoly position in landholding. The government's land policies resemble those of Stanford University: vast, potentially valuable holdings are allowed to lie fallow and are brought into productive use only at a remarkably slow pace.

The differences in government policies have led to dramatically different behavior of investment and the balance of international payments. Hong Kong's gross investment has been reasonably stable since 1960 at around 20 percent of GDP, and its current account has typically been near balance. Singapore's gross investment was 13 percent of GDP in the early 1960s, reached 21 percent between 1965 and 1969, and then soared to an average of nearly 40 percent since 1970. This staggering amount of investment has been financed partly by the highest saving rate in the world (thanks especially to governmental coercion) and, until the mid-1980s, by massive borrowing from abroad. Another way to put this is that Singapore's prosperity in terms of production has not been translated nearly as much as Hong Kong's into high levels of consumption. In 1990, when Singapore's per capita GDP was 104 percent of Hong Kong's, its per capita private consumption was only 71 percent of Hong Kong's.

Professor Alwyn Young of MIT's Sloan School showed (in the National Bureau of Economic Research's 1992 *Macroeconomic Annual*) what the different governmental policies have meant for productivity and growth. The main findings follow from the facts already presented: although Singapore has plowed twice as much of its GDP into investment, the growth rates of per capita GDP have been about the same. Singapore, in other words, has gotten much less out of each unit of investment. This relatively low return involves two elements. First, there has been so much investment that the real rate of return on capital has fallen sharply, and second, the growth of productivity (output per unit of quality-adjusted labor and capital) in Singapore has been much slower than in Hong Kong.

Professor Young attributes Singapore's low productivity growth to its industrial policy of picking winners to target for investment. The problem has not been so much the choice of the wrong winners but rather the tendency to select new winners too often. Since the late 1960s, Singapore has shifted from a trading post economy that had a large role for the British military and nonexport-oriented manufacturing, to an emphasis on export-oriented textiles and clothing, petroleum refining, various electronic products, computers, and financial services. It is apparently now targeting biotechnology and striving to become the Asian center for corporate headquarters. All of this in twenty-five years in a country of around 3 million persons. Apparently the Singaporeans have never stayed in one area long enough to gain the full extent of the productive efficiencies that result from learning and experience.

I should recall that this discussion concerns two of the great success stories among the world's economies. Hong Kong and Singapore are co-champions in growth rates of per capita GDP since 1960, and these performances reflect many favorable elements, such as friendly economic climates and political stability. Singapore's shortcomings have to be interpreted relative to Hong Kong's strengths, not relative to the many economic disaster areas of the developing world.

A fair conclusion, however, is that Singapore's forced saving and industrial targeting have been mistakes. Thus, these aspects of its policies should not be taken as lessons for the many less-developed countries that aspire to the growth performances achieved in East Asia.

The Optimal Size of a Nation, or the Attractions of Secession

The U.S. government is instinctively opposed to secession. It did not support the independence movements of the Kurds in Iraq, the Croats in Yugoslavia, the Ibos in Nigeria, or the Quebecois in Canada. The United States was pretty much the last major country to sign on to sovereignty for the Baltic states and delayed its endorsement of independence of the other Soviet republics. Thus, the U.S. government has been resistant to secession even when it involves an oppressed minority that joined up involuntarily and that would likely form a democratic government that would be friendly toward the United States and conducive to economic growth.

There seem to be two main reasons for this opposition. The first is the stability issue related to the potential trouble from changing borders. This view suggests that even borders that were drawn in an unreasonable manner—such as in Yugoslavia, Iraq, and much of Africa—may reasonably be defended because the process of change involves disruptions, including the possibility of Bosnian- or Chechnyan-style armed conflict. Of course, the attempt to maintain unsatisfactory boundaries may cause even more disruption.

Stability is a sensible concern, but the intense opposition of the U.S. government to secession also reflects the specifics of American history. The U.S. Civil War, by far the most costly conflict ever for the United States, was fought primarily to maintain the union. The war caused over 600,000 military fatalities and an unknown number of civilian deaths, and it severely damaged the southern economy. Per capita income went from about 80 percent of the northern level before the war (using the sketchy data available for 1840) to about 40 percent after the war (based on the more complete figures for 1880). The fall in per capita income reflected the destruction of capital—plant and equipment, livestock, and educated labor—and the end of the plantation system based on forced labor. Although only the first part of the fall in measured per capita income represents a true cost of the war, the overall setback to the economy was striking: it took more than a century after the war's end in 1865 for southern per capita income to reattain 80 percent of the northern level. This rate of convergence of the poor South to the rich North may seem slow, but the pace is typical of regional growth processes observed in other times and places; it reflects the iron-law of convergence.

If the U.S. government had supported the right of secession in some other part of the world, such as the Soviet Union, then it would have indirectly challenged the basic premise of the Civil War. Why was it desirable for Soviet republics to have the right to secession and undesirable for U.S. states to have the same rights? Americans would then be forced to reconsider whether the enormous cost of the Civil War in terms of lives and incomes was worth it. Instead of being the greatest of American presidents, as many people believe, Abraham Lincoln may instead have presided over the largest error in American history.

Although the desire to free the slaves was not the primary cause of the Civil War, one might argue that the elimination of this disgraceful oppression nevertheless made the war worthwhile. Two problems with this argument are, first, that the setback to the southern economy harmed the southern blacks along with the whites and, second, that the elimination of slavery did not prevent blacks from suffering through nearly an additional century of semilegal discrimination and segregation after the end of Reconstruction in the 1870s. Everyone would have been better off if the elimination of slavery had been accomplished by buying off the slaveowners—as the British did with the West Indian slaves during the 1830s—instead of fighting the war. Whether the blacks would have been better or worse off if the North had accepted the secession of the South requires a forecast of how the institution of slavery would have fared in an independent South. Some relevant information is that slavery was abolished without wars in the other parts of the Western Hemisphere (except for Haiti in the 1790s) and the last country to act, Brazil, began the process in 1871 and finished it in 1888. Thus, the experience of the rest of the hemisphere suggests that slavery in the U.S. South would have been eliminated peacefully in not very many years.

If we put the experience of the Civil War behind us and also abstract from the transitional problems of redrawing borders—that is, the stability issue—then the evaluation of a secession depends on whether, starting from scratch, reasonable borders would have been drawn very differently from those that currently prevail. Some of the arguments that have been used in this context to criticize the breakup of states are wrong and ought to be dismissed. For example, it is often stated that a potential new state is too small to be economically viable: Soviet Georgia or Croatia—or Quebec or Catalonia—could not make it on its own. The empirical evidence about the economic growth of countries conflicts sharply with this view. There is no relation between the growth or level of per capita income and the size of a country, measured by population or area. Small countries, even of populations as little as a million, can perform well economically, as long as they remain open to international trade. In fact, smallness tends to encourage openness because the alternative really would be a nonviable economy.

A related specious argument is that a state cannot prosper if it lacks a key natural resource, such as oil or fertile land. The experience with economic growth across countries reveals little relation between economic performance and the presence of natural resources. For example, Japan and the Asian tigers, as well as most of Western Europe, have done fine without domestic sources of oil. With access to international markets, a country can specialize in what it does well and then trade its goods for the commodities, such as oil or agricultural products, that it lacks domestically.

A characteristic that does promote economic growth is good government in the sense of maintenance of property rights, avoidance of trade barriers, and absence of other market distortions, including excessive tax rates and regulations. Thus, in evaluating a change of international borders, a key issue from an economic standpoint is whether the new government would be better or worse in terms of these growth-promoting activities. The Baltic states, Slovenia, and Croatia are examples in which secession led to more favorable government policies. (Bosnia and Northern Ireland are more difficult cases because the opposing ethnic groups are fighting for the same territory.) As another example, the breakup of Czechoslovakia into the Czech Republic and Slovakia has improved public policies in the former country and possibly also in the latter country.

Although it may be an unpleasant commentary on human nature, a central driving force in defining a state is the desire to have a reasonably homogeneous population within its borders. It is clear, for example, from observing the places where secessionist movements tend to occur, such as Yugoslavia and the former Soviet Union or Spain and Canada, that ethnic identity is a central driving force. There are cases in which governments have dealt more or less successfully with sharp ethnic diversities, such as Switzerland and even the United States or Belgium, but the problems are easier to pinpoint than the triumphs.

Political economy explains some of the benefits from having a reasonably homogeneous population within a given state. If diversity is great—measured, say, by the inequality in potential earnings—then there is a strong incentive for people to spend their energies in efforts to redistribute income rather than to produce goods. In particular, a greater dispersion of constituent characteristics leads to the creation of interest groups that spend their time lobbying the central government to redistribute resources in their favor. In a democracy, this process involves voter behavior, whereas in a dictatorship the pressures from interest groups are less direct. But either way, excessive diversity of preferences encourages people to expend resources in unproductive ways and leads thereby to poor economic performance.

We can think of a country's optimal size as emerging from a trade-off: a large country can spread the cost of public goods, such as defining a legal and monetary system and maintaining national security, over many taxpayers, but a large country is also likely to have a diverse population that is difficult for the central government to satisfy. The reason that small countries perform reasonably well in practice is that the public-goods argument may not be so important. For instance, a larger country has more property to protect from foreign aggressors and therefore requires larger outlays for national defense than a small country. Empirically, the ratio of defense expenditures to GDP is uncorrelated with the size of the country: if the public-goods argument were compelling, then larger countries would tend to spend less on defense as a share of GDP. No doubt, it is inefficient for sovereign states to be too small, but the minimum size for a viable state seems not to be very great.

The bottom line is that political separation is sometimes a good idea: the benefits can outweigh the losses, including the transitional costs of changing borders. Hence, the U.S. government should avoid knee-jerk opposition to secession and should instead support separatist movements on a selective basis. A key ingredient is the presence of an oppressed minority that would likely install an improved, democratic government. Using this guideline, some past cases that warranted U.S. support—at least in terms of recognition—were the Croats, the Kurds, and the peoples of the various Soviet republics.

Europe's Road to Serfdom: A Perspective on European Union

Opinion polls in Europe in 1992 and thereafter showed sharp divisions about the wisdom of further European unification. Moreover, the extent of involvement in Europe is a continuing source of bitter dispute in the United Kingdom, where another referendum is likely to come in the future. This debate is reasonable because further integration—including coordination of fiscal policies to facilitate the adoption of a single currency—amounts to additional steps toward a centralized European government based in Brussels. Not surprisingly, such steps appeal mainly to people who like large, centralized government.

Some economists argue from basically an engineering perspective that the unification of currencies is efficient. A single currency avoids the transaction costs and uncertainties involved with the exchange of one money for another. From this standpoint, the argument for a unified currency is analogous to the case for a common language. Settlement on a single language (hopefully English) would eliminate the costs associated with translation. The savings on transaction costs would, in fact, be far greater than those generated from a move to a common currency. We observe, however, that small nations are often willing to bear high costs to maintain or promote their distinct languages, such as Catalan in Catalonia (well publicized since the Barcelona Olympics in 1992) or French in Quebec. This willingness indicates that groups of persons with a common heritage attach significant benefits to having their own language. Much smaller benefits from individual currencies would be enough to outweigh the saving in transaction costs from moving to a single currency.

Unfortunately, the main case that economists have made against monetary unification (and similarly against a regime of fixed exchange rates without capital controls) is the Keynesian argument for the benefit of independent monetary policies. An economy that experiences a recession is supposed to value the opportunity to print a lot of money to stimulate the economy, and monetary unification eliminates this option. According to this argument, Massachusetts would have benefited greatly in the late 1980s if it could have printed a lot of Massachusetts greenbacks to counter the downturn in its economy. A more serious analysis of the Massachusetts situation suggests that real factors were involved—shifts of industry mix away from defense and computers, high state tax rates, and the decline of the national economy—and that money creation would not have been helpful. More generally, economists have been recognizing that the main function of monetary policy is to provide an underlying stable framework for the economy, not to attempt to fine-tune the business cycle. This outlook suggests that the benefits from independent monetary policies would be minor at best.

A more important criticism of monetary unification is that it contributes to the centralization of government more broadly: it represents a repression of national identity that could also be applied to language, culture, the extent of public-sector activity, and so on. The appeal of a single currency is like the superficial attraction of central planning. A single monetary authority is thought to eliminate the unnecessary transaction costs from the existence of competing currencies in the first instance, whereas the social planner is thought to remove the wasteful duplication from market competition in the second case. In both situations, the benefits from central planning are exaggerated, and the rewards from competition are underestimated.

Proponents of a strong central government sometimes argue that chaos results from the uncoordinated policies of individual governments, for example, from fifty state governments instead of the U.S. federal government. Such arguments have been used to rationalize and advance the centralization of governmental power in the United States. This concentration of power loses the benefits from competition among governments and also precludes a good match between public policies and the preferences of the residents of the individual states. Each state government can, for example, choose different levels of spending on education and welfare, different policies on drugs and crime, and—if the Supreme Court would allow it—different regulations on abortion. The apparent chaos from this diversity should instead be viewed as a reasonably good match between public policies and the desires of residents.

The central issue is the optimal size of a country and, as a related matter, the optimal range of application of a language or a currency. Empirical observation suggests the desirability of avoiding the two extremes: a single world government with one language and one currency and a proliferation of thousands of countries, each with its own media of speech and exchange. Languages and currencies would not be very useful if each person used his or her own specialized medium, but the desirability of full coordination is also doubtful.

Large countries can secure the benefits from reduced costs of public goods, and a common language and currency are two examples of these benefits. The costs of larger countries involve the increased potential for government-sponsored monopoly power and the decreasing likelihood that centralized decisions can be matched with the differing wants of more diversified constituents. In some cases, outcomes would be better if countries became smaller and if government policies thereby became better matched to the characteristics of their populations. These arguments can rationalize the kinds of secessions that have recently become popular, although the process of separation sometimes entails violence and other costs. These costs can be attributed now to the act of secession, but they can just as well be ascribed to unwise unifications—forms of forced integration—that took place in the past. One drawback from excessive unification, such as the plans for bringing the European countries closer together, is the high cost of dissolving these linkages later.

A similar perspective applies to various international organizations that seek to perform governmental functions that extend beyond the boundaries of single countries. The United Nations, for example, strives to perform some functions of a world government, and some observers think that it would be desirable if this kind of institution made numerous global decisions on environmental regulation, energy production, redistribution of income between rich and poor countries, choices about war and peace, and so on. If a single European currency is a good idea, then why not go forward to a world currency managed by a central bank stationed at the United Nations?

Before we get carried away along these lines of globally centralized government, we ought to worry about how well the United Nations and other international organizations have been handling their existing tasks. In many cases, small is beautiful is a better guide to the appropriate jurisdiction and range of functions of government.

Default on Sovereign Debt

"Money for nothing" is an old idea as a basis for economic development. The most common form is foreign aid, a program that has been a notable failure in Africa, South Asia, and elsewhere. Another manifestation is the supposed benefits to developing countries from default (or "rescheduling") of their sovereign foreign debts. If only a country can escape from its onerous debt burdens—as in such past cases as Mexico, Brazil, Poland, and Russia—then the claim is that development prospects would be greatly enhanced.

In 1991, an especially ambitious money-for-nothing proposal involved a "grand bargain" with Russia, whereby $150 billion in aid over five years would somehow be linked to meaningful economic reforms. Many observers expressed skepticism about whether such linkage was feasible, whether Western aid would provide any stimulus to reforms, and whether significant economic improvements in Russia were possible in any event. But even if the prospects for economic advance were bright, it would remain unclear that the West ought to pay for it.

The transition from socialistic to capitalistic economic organization amounts to a high-return investment that likely requires some reduction of output in the short run. Reforms in Russia or other transforming economies could be financed by national saving, but the transition would be facilitated by access to international loans and direct foreign investments. The problem, however, is that potential lenders and investors rationally fear that the Russians and other debtors will default on loans and expropriate foreign-owned properties. For this reason, profit-oriented international loans and investments tend to be limited, and the focus often shifts to gifts from developed countries and international organizations.

One interpretation of the proposed grand bargain with Russia is that the United States and the other main developed countries should provide gifts because large-scale private lending is not an option. The past behavior of the U.S. and other governments in failing to enforce international loan contracts has something to do with the exclusion of many developing countries from world credit markets, and the strengthening of these markets would be more useful than foreign aid. But another suggestion is that the main quid pro quo for our gifts would be the maintenance of a peaceful Russia, a situation that allows for lower defense outlays in the West.

But is it obvious that a more efficient Russian economy would lessen the external threat? One reason the threat has diminished in recent years is that the deterioration of the economy has reduced the resources available for the Russian military. Looking ahead, a move to a productive market economy would have two effects. First, the increase in resources (due to higher productivity or to Western aid) would raise the funds available for military purposes. But second, the maintenance of a stable internal political system and the creation of market arrangements geared to private property and consumer products would, it is hoped, lead to a less belligerent stance. The second force may eventually dominate, but it would be foolhardy for the West to count on it. For instance, during World War II, Germany and Japan were capitalistic economies. Would we have been better or worse off if those economies had been more efficient?

The question of gifts from the West to Russia and other places would probably not arise if developing countries had good access to well-functioning credit markets. These markets have been harmed by the frequent defaults of sovereign borrowers, often supported by the U.S. and other governments. For example, the United States was instrumental in the debt reschedulings in Latin America. Instead of encouraging defaults and easy bankruptcies, the best thing that the U.S. government could have done for world development over the past twenty-five years would have been to use all legal means, including seizures of foreign goods, to ensure the repayment of legitimate international claims. It is only this kind of tough enforcement policy by lenders that ensures access to credit by poor countries (or poor individuals). Although some countries gained in the short run by defaulting on obligations, most would have been better off in the long run by maintaining access to credit markets.

Alexander Hamilton understood these points when he stressed the importance of the U.S. federal government's honoring the various colonial debts incurred during the American Revolution. Only this strong credit record would ensure that the new nation would retain access to borrowing over its long period of economic development. The leaders of developing countries, as well as those of the main creditor nations, would do well to reread the words of Hamilton.

Democracy and Growth in Peru

In April 1992, President Alberto Fujimori of Peru dismissed the legislature and unilaterally expanded the scope of his executive authority. The U.S. secretary of state at the time, James Baker, reacted to this coup by saying, "You cannot destroy democracy in order to save it." Mr. Baker was wrong about Peru: the economic and political situation was sufficiently desperate that President Fujimori's iron hand represented the only hope for improvement.

Peru was not in bad shape economically in the mid-1970s. In 1975, its real per capita GDP was about the same as Chile's, one-third higher than Ecuador's, and nearly twice that of Paraguay's, then the lowest in South America. In contrast Peru's per capita GDP in 1990 was less than half Chile's, 20 percent below Ecuador's, and 10 percent less than Paraguay's.

Peru's weak performance in the early 1980s (per capita growth of −3 percent per year from 1980 to 1985) can be attributed to the worldwide recession, but the collapse of the late 1980s (per capita growth of −5 percent per year from 1985 to 1990) must be credited to the socialistic policies of the former president, Alan García. Mr. García's view was that the more regulations and the more central planning and government spending, the better. He rapidly exhausted Peru's foreign reserves, created runaway inflation, and suspended most payments on the external debt. The burdens from licensing requirements, bureaucratic regulations, and political corruption made Peru a place in which it was virtually impossible for businesses to participate in the formal market sector.

The constraint on legitimate activity was illustrated by an experiment reported by Hernando De Soto in his book, *The Other Path*. He found that it took nearly a year of filling out forms and seeking licenses to open a small business in Lima. Although he sought not to pay bribes, such payments were requested ten times and had to be paid on two occasions in order to proceed even after a delay.

The withdrawal of economic activity from the formal sector in Peru led to a plunge in tax revenues, and the government's response of raising tax rates led to further withdrawals—a striking example of the Laffer curve (whereby higher tax rates can lead to lower tax revenues). By the end of the García administration in 1990, the government's tax collections were a mere 4 percent of GDP, despite the presence of high tax rates.

Mr. Fujimori received less than 25 percent of the vote in the first round of the 1990 election but was the surprise winner against the center-right coalition candidate, Mario Vargas Llosa, in the second round. It was only after the election that President Fujimori adopted the reasonable reforms that had been advocated by his opponent. Government subsidies and other expenditures were then cut, foreign trade was liberalized, payments on the foreign debt were resumed, strict monetary control was observed, the inflation rate fell dramatically, and tax receipts rose by early 1992 to 8 percent of GDP.

Mr. Fujimori, whose party controlled only 21 percent of the seats in the legislature after the 1990 elections, encountered increasing legislative opposition in his efforts to privatize government enterprises, reduce the size of the governmental bureaucracy, and apply a 5 percent sales tax to the vast informal sector of the economy. The opposition stemmed especially from Mr. García's APRA party, a group that had a vested interest in the government jobs and privileges granted by the preceding administration. The APRA party hoped, in particular, to return to power in 1995, an outcome that would have led to a repeat of the disastrous socialistic policies of the late 1980s.

The extent of the economic emergency and the political impasse represented by the interest groups that opposed reforms might, by themselves, have constituted reasonable grounds for a suspension of democracy. But the decisive element was the struggle against the terrorist group, the Shining Path. This group's intimidation of judges and legislators and its collusion with the prison administration had rendered ineffective the usual procedures of rules of evidence, eligibility for parole, and levels of punishment. The extent of the crisis became clear in early 1992 when the supreme court ruled that there was insufficient evidence to bring to trial Abimael Guzman, the leader of the Shining Path. Most Peruvians reacted with outrage and with the conviction that the situation amounted to a wartime emergency that called for strong executive powers with close military support. This belief explains the extent of the popular support for Mr. Fujimori's seizure of power.

It is worth noting as a longer-term lesson that the key source of the Shining Path's economic power was the U.S. government's drug policy. The Peruvian terrorists obtained most of their income from the protective services that they provided to local drug traffickers. American aid to Peru, earmarked mostly for drug interdiction, created more demand for these protective services and thereby added to the Shining Path's income. The U.S. government could have achieved pretty much the same result if it had given the aid money directly to the terrorists. More fundamentally, the problems stemmed from the demand for drugs by U.S. residents in conjunction with the U.S. government's policy of curtailing the supply of drugs by making the trade illegal and dangerous. If drugs were legalized, then the demand for the Shining Path's protective services would have vanished along with its income (as would the incomes of many criminals in the United States).

Peru's situation can be compared with some other Latin American countries that have used less drastic political means to move away from socialism and toward free markets. Mexico successfully instituted privatization and the opening of markets without reducing political rights. But the Mexican reforms were instituted by a monopoly political party, and the government did not have to counter a major terrorist threat. (The Mexican problems with Chiapas do not compare with those of the Shining Path.)

Argentina, after several decades of failed policies, carried out economic reforms within the context of democratic rule. But unlike Peru, the situation involved no terrorist threat. Also, the fragility of the Argentine political situation still makes the durability of the reforms uncertain.

In the 1970s, Chile instituted admirable moves toward a free market, but this economic liberalization was accompanied by many years of President Pinochet's constraints on political expression and civil liberties. The objective in Peru in 1992 was to follow the Chilean examples on economic reform while drastically compressing the transition back to democracy. Pinochet with a human face is perhaps a fair description of the desired policy.

President Fujimori argued persuasively in 1992 that a suspension of democracy—in effect, a peaceful revolution—was essential to revamp the government and thereby undertake a successful attack on terrorism and the problems of the economy. He also proposed a timetable for a return to democracy along with the elimination of terrorism and the institution of market reforms. The program was provisionally accepted in 1992 by Japan (Peru's largest source of external aid), a reasoned response that made Secretary Baker's knee-jerk, adverse reaction look embarrassing. Mr. Fujimori's actions also received a 70 to 90 percent approval rating in Peruvian opinion polls in 1992, a remarkably favorable reception considering that he received less than one-quarter of the vote in the initial round of the 1990 election and that only one-fifth of the legislature belonged to his party.

In 1992, Mr. Fujimori deserved a chance to show that his program could work and would not be a long-term departure from democratic rule. He deserved provisional U.S. support, a support that could best have been expressed not in terms of foreign aid or suspension of debt payments but rather by a change in drug policy. For the United States, the best approach to the drug problem poses difficult choices. But for Peru and several other countries in South America, the choice of the best policy is clear: for the United States to legalize drugs.

The Aftermath of Mr. Fujimori's Self-Revolution*

Despite the heavy U.S. criticism of President Fujimori's dissolution of congress in April 1992, the move turned out to be a great success in terms of economic reforms, reductions of terrorism, and the restoration of democracy. In September 1992, the leader of the Shining Path, Abimael Guzman, was captured, an act that marked a decisive downturn in the terrorist movement in Peru. In November 1992, President Fujimori's party won a strong majority in the newly elected congress, whose first responsibility was to write a new constitution. This document, approved through a public referendum in October 1993, eliminated much of the socialist philosophy of the old constitution while strengthening commitments to free markets and property rights. In a more activist mode, the new constitution also made guarantees about public education and the provision of information about market goods, health, and safety.

The legal changes were accompanied by dramatic reforms that freed up the financial sector, foreign trade, and labor markets. There was also a major privatization program, improve-

---

* Dr. Norman Loayza of the World Bank assisted in the preparation of this material.

ments in the security of property rights, establishment of a private pension scheme, reform of the tax system, and elimination of price controls and public monopolies. The resulting economic performance was strong, including a move to near price stability and a growth rate for real GDP in 1994 of 13 percent.

On the political front, Mr. Fujimori followed through in April 1995 on his promise of free general elections, and he won reelection with a strong 64 percent of the vote. (He has therefore managed in the past five years to defeat two rivals with equally surprising credentials: Mario Vargas Llosa, a novelist, in the 1990 elections and Javier Perez de Cuellar, a former U.N. secretary general, in the 1995 elections.) In addition to his personal victory, Mr. Fujimori's party won an absolute majority in the new congress.

By 1995, Peru was one of the more promising countries in terms of economic prospects. Moreover, its democracy had not only been restored but appeared much more stable than before the peaceful coup of April 1992. Thus, in sharp contrast to the U.S. opinion at the time, it apparently was possible in Peru to "destroy democracy in order to save it."

2

Monetary and Financial Policy

Argentina and Mexico: Latin Lessons in Monetary Policy

Argentina and Mexico have made major progress recently in economic reforms, notably in privatization, the structure of the public finances, and liberalization of foreign trade. The reforms were also supposed to include movements toward price stability, reinforced in each case by a commitment to maintain the value of the currency in U.S. dollars. In this context, Argentina has succeeded while Mexico has failed.

For Argentina, the soundness of the currency is guaranteed by the convertibility law (1 peso = 1 U.S. dollar) and the central bank's charter, which requires full backing of the monetary base by international reserves. Some questions arise about the definition of these reserves (whether they should include a small quantity of dollar-denominated government bonds and whether they should subtract obligations to international organizations), but the important point is that changes in the monetary base have been closely linked to the balance of payments. Thus, figure 3 shows that the movements in the base since 1991 have nearly matched the variations in international reserves. In this sense, the Argentine monetary system has functioned as a currency board.

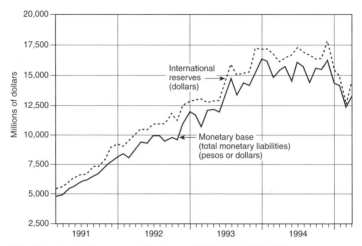

Note: End–of–month figures, except latest value plotted is for April 11, 1995.

Figure 3
International reserves and monetary base in Argentina. Source: Central
Bank of Argentina.

(A currency board is an arrangement whereby the monetary
authority issues paper currency notes only at a fixed rate of
exchange with a designated reserve medium, such as gold or a
specified foreign currency. The domestic quantity of money in
the form of currency rises only when people bring to the
authority an equally valued amount of reserves, and the
domestic quantity of currency falls only when people bring
back these notes to exchange for reserves. If the monetary
authority begins with reserves that are at least equal in value to
its outstanding currency, then it always has enough reserves to
buy back all of this currency at the designated exchange rate.
Therefore, it can always maintain the exchange rate between
currency and reserves as long as it never cheats by using
reserves to buy something other than its currency. Problems

can arise, however, if the authority uses reserves for other purposes, for example, to make loans to governments or private banks.)

Speculative reactions to the Mexican financial crisis led to a sharp decline in Argentina's reserves from December 1994 to March 1995 and, in accordance with currency board rules, to a fall by one-quarter in the monetary base. This willingness to endure a severe monetary contraction underscored the government's commitment to the value of its currency. The monetary contraction was not reversed until April, in response to growing confidence that the government was serious about maintaining the value of the peso (a view that was reinforced by loan commitments from international organizations and private banks). Ironically, the key element behind this confidence may be Argentina's history of high and volatile inflation. In this environment, any devaluation would immediately reduce the government's credibility to zero, and the general awareness of this fact makes it rational to believe that the government will stick to its promises.

Mexico's reform plan also included a fixed exchange rate, but the government and the central bank never had a clear monetary policy in place to maintain this rate. Figure 4 shows that from early 1991 until November 1994—a period that includes the presidential election in August 1994 and the turmoil that preceded the election—international reserves always exceeded the monetary base. (In the figure, the base has been converted from pesos into dollars at a hypothetically fixed exchange rate of 3.0, the value that applied in early 1991.) But the relation between movements in reserves and changes in the base was nil, because the central bank engaged in offsetting operations to insulate domestic monetary conditions from the balance of payments. In particular, expansions or contractions

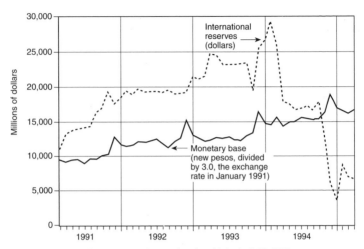

Note: End–of–month figures , except latest value plotted is for April 12, 1995.

Figure 4
International reserves and monetary base in Mexico. Source: Central Bank of Mexico.

of international reserves were associated, respectively, with reductions or increases in the bank's domestic credit.

Until November 1994, the divorce of the monetary base from international reserves was not necessarily inconsistent with the maintenance of a fixed exchange rate. Surplus reserves could be exchanged for domestic assets, and vice versa, but the reserves always provided full cover for the monetary base. In November and December, however, investors lost confidence in Mexico's commitment to a fixed exchange rate, and a run on international reserves ensued.

One negative element was the report on November 23 of likely high-level involvement in the assassination of a well-known politician in September. But more significant was the announcement on November 30 of the new cabinet, notably the absence of Pedro Aspe, the key economic thinker of the outgoing government, and the presence of a lesser-known person as finance minister. This unfortunate change of personnel was followed in December by the government's hesitation and vacillation on whether to devalue. Thus, the identity and pronouncements of the new government were important factors that helped to persuade the financial markets that the commitment to maintain the exchange rate was no longer serious.

Another key matter from late November through mid-December was the policy of the central bank. With reserves no longer in surplus, the fixed exchange rate could be guaranteed only if the plunge of reserves was matched by a decline in the monetary base (of the sort that occurred in Argentina from December 1994 to March 1995). Instead, the bank continued its policy of sterilization, so that the drop in foreign assets was balanced by a dramatic increase of domestic credit, not by a fall in the monetary base. As Figure 4 shows, one cannot even detect from the behavior of the base after October 1994 that a financial crisis was going on. The base exhibited its usual seasonal rise in December and showed no signs overall of contraction. (Things could have been worse; the monetary base could have been sharply increased.)

As a technical matter, it is always feasible to peg the exchange rate if the central bank starts with reserves in excess of the monetary base (the bank's monetary liabilities) and if the bank pays out or receives reserves only in exchange for monetary base at the fixed rate. That is why a currency board fails only when the authority deviates from the rules.

Problems arise if the central bank tries to maintain not only the foreign currency value of its monetary liabilities but also the obligations of other sectors, notably government and private banks. Specifically, the vast expansion of the central bank's domestic credit after October 1994 appears to be an attempt to maintain the dollar value of government bonds and bank deposits—that is, to avoid increases in interest rates, as well as defaults by government and banks.

The central bank's reserves were sufficient to cover the monetary base but not nearly enough to match the sum of government bonds and broad monetary aggregates. Thus, once the financial markets reduced their dollar valuation of Mexican assets, the bank's pursuit of this broader, unrealistic goal only encouraged the run on reserves by making devaluation inevitable. In the end, the desire to stabilize the dollar value of too many obligations led to a depreciation of anything that was fixed in peso terms.

Countries do not, of course, have to run their monetary systems by pegging an exchange rate. Mexico could, for example, have floated the currency in the fall of 1994 and then geared its monetary policy toward domestic price stability (essentially the ongoing policy of the United States).

The advantage of a fixed exchange rate is that it provides external discipline in a way that is closely monitored by financial markets. This discipline is more important—and the success of a domestically oriented monetary policy is less probable—the worse the country's history with respect to delivering price stability and honoring financial obligations. For Argentina, the sorry history of high and volatile inflation made critical the maintenance of the fixed exchange rate. For Mexico, the past performance of inflation and default was poor, but perhaps not bad enough to make unthinkable the devaluation of December 1994. It also did not help that the Mexicans knew that they could run down their reserves and then count on a vast financial bailout from the United States and the International Monetary Fund.

It became fashionable in 1995 to blame the outgoing Mexican administration—notably President Salinas and Finance Minister Aspe—for the financial crisis. The previous government did make some mistakes. One error was the sharp expansion of loans to private banks in 1993–1994. This flow rose to 4 percent of gross domestic product (GDP) but was not counted in the fiscal deficit, because the loans were classed as acquisitions of assets by the government.

Another mistake was the rolling over of government debt primarily into short-term obligations, in order to avoid the payment of high interest rates on long-term debt. Refunding costs thereby became highly sensitive to shifts in market sentiment. (The old government was also criticized for denominating much of its debt in U.S. dollars, a procedure that was intended to underscore the commitment to a fixed exchange rate. This procedure was fine until the new government rediscovered the superficial attractions of devaluation.)

Finally, it would have been desirable for the central bank to shift toward a contractionary policy in March 1994, when an earlier political assassination—this time of the main party's presidential candidate—led to a sharp loss of international reserves. Although reserves were still $18 billion in April 1994—more than the monetary base—a monetary contraction in late March would have stemmed the loss of reserves and helped to reinforce the commitment to the fixed exchange rate.

Despite these errors, the outgoing administration had built up a solid reputation with the financial markets, specifically in regard to maintaining the value of the currency. Thus, a reasonable view is that the speculation in fall 1994 against the Mexican currency would not have occurred if people had expected the old government—at least Finance Minister Aspe—to remain in power. (President Salinas's continuation in office was precluded by the Mexican constitution.) Moreover, the previous administration probably would have persuaded the "independent" central bank to respond by December 1994 in the appropriate contractionary manner—along Argentinean lines—rather than with full sterilization. The central bank and the new government did not want the contraction because they did not want a recession—but the policy of devaluation and foreign bailout did not avoid this outcome.

Pedro Aspe has this to say about credibility (in his 1993 book, *Economic Transformation the Mexican Way*): "Credibility is not a gift—it has to be earned. It is built up one step at a time and supported by facts, and by consistency. Even more, credibility is never owned; it is rented, because it can be taken away at any time." Mr. Aspe worked hard as finance minister to build up Mexico's credibility, but it was all lost in December 1994, and it is unclear to what extent and when it will be regained. Argentina not only maintained its credibility during the crisis that began in December 1994 but strengthened it by weathering a great storm. It is a case of two countries that began on similar paths but then moved in very different directions.

Monetary Policy: A Matter of Commitment

Monetary policy controls nominal variables: in level form, the price level, monetary aggregates, the exchange rate, and nominal GDP; in rate-of-change form, the inflation rate, nominal interest rates, and growth rates of money, exchange rates, and nominal GDP. Monetary policy has uncertain, and usually short-lived and minor, influences over the main real variables, such as real exchange rates, real GDP, and real interest rates.

The central bank's principal mission ought to be to control nominal variables so as to provide for a stable framework within which the private economy gets accurate signals and can therefore make efficient allocations of resources. Many countries have recently accepted this idea by adopting some version of price stability as an objective.

One version of this objective is the minimization of departures of an index of the general price level from a prespecified path, which could be a constant. In this arrangement, the monetary authority makes up for past mistakes on inflation; for example, if the inflation rate is above target for awhile, then it has to be below target (and possible negative) later to return to the desired price level. The gold standard and a fixed exchange rate (such as Argentina's present system) are examples of this type of regime.

Alternatively, the central bank can manage its monetary instruments to minimize surprise movements in the price level while also targeting the inflation rate. In this arrangement, past mistakes on inflation are bygones, which do not call for future policy adjustments. The present U.S. monetary policy seems to be an example of this system.

One advantage of the first type of regime is that the targeting of the price level facilitates long-term nominal contracts, which require confidence about the value of money in the long run. The second type of regime exhibits "price-level drift," because the failure to correct for previous mistakes on inflation means that the price level can wander anywhere in the long run. However, if the inflation rate is guided by a fixed target in each period, then the rate at which this drift can occur is limited.

A disadvantage of the first kind of system is that it sometimes requires corrective actions that are themselves very costly; for example, the economy would have to endure an extended deflation to make up for a prior inflation. Moreover, if the monetary authority were unwilling to engineer this deflation (presumably because the public would not tolerate it), then the credibility of the entire system is threatened.

The choice between the two approaches to price stability is unclear. However, either set-up is preferable to arrangements, prevalent in the 1960s and 1970s, in which governments made no commitment at all to low inflation. Thus, the more basic question is, What mechanism will ensure the credibility of the chosen program of monetary stability? If the central bank lacks some form of commitment, then it encounters a problem that has become familiar in the academic literature.

The problem arises because many policymakers and economists have two possibly correct beliefs. First, it is worthwhile in a recession to endure higher inflation to hold down the rise in unemployment. Second, the economy possesses a short-run "Phillips curve"; that is, higher rates of money growth and inflation lead temporarily to lower rates of unemployment. The existence of a Phillips curve over any time frame is controversial. In the long run, it is implausible that people would work harder and produce more goods and services just because prices are rising—and are expected to rise—at a faster rate. The idea behind the short-run Phillips curve is that people may be induced to work harder and produce more if the rates of increase of wages and prices are high in relation to the expectations that people formed over the past year or so. That is, monetary growth and inflation are thought to be expansionary when they are high in relation to the inflation to which the economy has become accustomed.

Armed with these two beliefs, the central bank would respond to an economic downturn with a monetary expansion. The problem is that this expansion of money growth and inflation would work to bolster the economy—if it ever works— only if it keeps ahead of expectations. More realistically, the monetary reactions would usually be anticipated; that is, people would understand the general nature of the policy and would adjust inflation expectations accordingly. In this case, the policy succeeds mainly in creating high and variable inflation, as in the United States from the late 1960s through the early 1980s.

Moreover, in a system without commitment, the monetary authority is caught in a dilemma. If people anticipate a monetary expansion in response to a recession and if the authority fails to validate this belief, then the recession would be exacerbated. Thus, it is not easy to avoid the problem by "just saying no." The only satisfactory way out is to institute a regime in which the monetary authority is committed to price stability. If this commitment is credible, then people do not expect monetary expansion in response to a recession, and the failure to create this expansion therefore does not exacerbate the recession.

One mechanism for implementing a commitment to price stability is the government's adoption of a formal rule of behavior. An example would be a promise to adhere to the gold standard or a fixed exchange rate. Other possibilities are a commitment to a particular plan for price stability or a monetary rule. The seriousness of the government's commitment would, as in other policy areas, depend on its form. Simple promises of public officials differ from statutes, which differ from constitutional provisions. In any of these contexts, the weight of the commitment—that is, the penalty imposed on broken promises—likely depends on the social consensus about the importance of the transgression. For example, inflation is taken especially seriously in Germany because of the past experience with hyperinflation. In Argentina, any violation of the country's convertibility law, which ensures the value of the peso in terms of the U.S. dollar, would have grave consequences because of the history of high and volatile inflation.

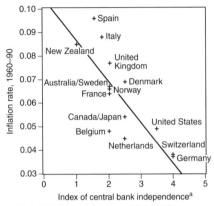

a. 1 is least independent; 4 is most independent.

Figure 5
Inflation and central bank independence. Source: Alesina and Summers 1992.

Another possibility, which is becoming increasingly popular, is to establish a central bank that is "guaranteed" to be independent of the government. The bank may have a charter that commits it to price stability or some related objective. Although the independence of a central bank from a sovereign government can never be complete, the degree of independence does vary across countries.

Studies of the major developed countries show that a less independent central bank tends to deliver higher and more variable inflation. Figure 5 shows some of this evidence. Notice that Switzerland, Germany, and the United States had the three most independent central banks and had average inflation rates from 1955 to 1988 of 3.2 percent, 3.0 percent, and 4.1 percent, respectively, whereas New Zealand, Spain, and Italy had the three least independent central banks and had average inflation rates of 7.6 percent, 8.5 percent, and 7.3 percent, respectively. (More recently, the New Zealand central bank received a new charter and has become one of the most independent in the world.)

The empirical results on central bank independence make sense because a less independent bank is more subject to political pressures to inflate the economy in response to a recession. This kind of inflation tends, if at all, to stimulate the economy only when it exceeds the inflation that people were expecting. Thus, the politically dependent central bank tries to set inflation systematically above expected inflation, an objective that violates Abraham Lincoln's famous dictum about the possibilities for fooling all of the people and that leads on average to high and volatile inflation. (Lincoln said, "You may fool all of the people some of the time; you can even fool some of the people all of the time.")

The higher and more variable inflation associated with less central bank independence might be worthwhile if it led to better economic performance. But the degree of bank independence turns out to be unrelated to the average rate of economic growth and the average unemployment rate. Thus, a move to a more independent central bank appears to be all gain and no pain.

The personality of the central bank governor may also matter when the bank has some degree of independence. In particular, an individual who detests inflation and cares little about unemployment delivers the same results as a person who is committed to low inflation. Thus, a hard-hearted governor can achieve good outcomes even from the standpoint of an observer who cares deeply about growth and unemployment. Similarly, it is desirable to choose a central bank governor who places a lot of value on kept promises—someone who really means it when he or she commits to price stability, no matter what.

It is also not important for the governor to be a good macroeconomist. For example, even if a short-run Phillips curve exists, it is better if the central banker believes otherwise and therefore thinks that inflation has no benefits, only costs. The higher the costs ascribed to inflation—even if they are irrational—the better the implied commitment to price stability.

The approach that stresses personality and character of policymakers tends to give Paul Volcker and Alan Greenspan a lot of credit for the restoration of monetary credibility in the United States after the disastrous increases in inflation and nominal interest rates during the late 1970s. This approach also implies that it makes a good deal of difference if appointments to the central bank are of individuals who are not strongly committed to low inflation.

To make the argument concrete, in spring 1994, President Clinton appointed Alan Blinder to be vice chairman of the Federal Reserve Board. The appointment appeared at the time to be a grooming for the chairmanship. If Alan Blinder had made it, which seemed unlikely in late 1995, he would probably have been the best academic economist ever to hold that position.

This is actually faint praise, given the academic credentials of past Fed chairmen. But the real question is whether the appointment of someone with strong academic qualifications would deliver good monetary policy. The appointment would be great if the central bank's principal task were the implementation of an optimal plan for fine-tuning the economy. A fine-tuner would carefully adjust monetary growth and interest rates in response to economic fluctuations so as to attain a desired trade-off between inflation and real variables, such as unemployment and the growth of real GDP. But, as already argued, the key aspect of a Fed chairman is the commitment to low inflation, not the ability to fine-tune.

The ideal central banker should always appear somber in public, never tell any jokes, and complain continually about the dangers of inflation. Thus, Paul Volcker and Alan Greenspan look good, and Arthur Burns seemed ideal until he supported President Nixon's use of price controls. Alan Blinder is, however, problematic. He has an excellent sense of humor, undoubtedly likes small children and defenseless animals, cares deeply about poor people, and clearly believes that expanding the money supply during a recession would, at least in the short run, lower the unemployment rate. With this belief in a short-run Phillips curve, there is no way that he would maintain a commitment to price stability when the economy's growth rate slows down. In other words, Alan Blinder is a nice person and a solid macroeconomist but has all the wrong traits for a central bank governor. The financial markets would never take him seriously.

I should report that my arguments about the significance of the Fed chairman's character and beliefs were challenged in a letter that I received from Milton Friedman. Milton says, in part:

I am much less confident than you that the personality of the Chairman of the Fed and his demeanor makes much difference except as it is itself a reflection of the President's attitudes. I believe that Volcker was successful in the early 1980s in ending inflation not because of his demeanor, not because of his personal character, but because Ronald Reagan did not object and backed him. It is my conviction that when push comes to shove the President will always get his way regardless of who is running the Federal Reserve. If in late 1995 or early 1996 the economy is starting to look very shaky and threatening to interfere with Clinton's reelection prospects, I predict that we will have an inflationary monetary stimulus regardless of who is Chairman, regardless of whether Alan Greenspan is reappointed to another term or whether Alan Blinder becomes the Chairman. On the other hand, I also predict that if the economy continues to do very well, if its behavior along with low inflation looks favorable for Clinton's reelection, there will be no such inflationary burst, again regardless of who is Chairman.

I suppose that the key evidence I would cite for this conclusion is Arthur Burns. As you know, when he was named Chairman, I thought he was the right person in the right place at the right time as I wrote in a *Newsweek* column. I turned out to be wrong. It was not that Arthur was insufficiently dour; it was not because he did not understand what the effects of monetary growth would be. It was because President Nixon wanted badly to get reelected and was willing to take whatever chances were necessary for that purpose. That was why Arthur went along with wage and price controls.

As indicated by the references to Arthur Burns, Milton has changed his views about the significance of the individuals who lead the Federal Reserve. In *The Monetary History of the United States*, Milton Friedman and Anna Schwartz made the opposite argument when they contended that the death in 1928 of Benjamin Strong, the governor of the New York Federal Reserve Bank, was a key ingredient in the Great Depression.

No doubt the significance of individuals in the conduct of monetary policy or in history more broadly will not be settled here. I should report, however, on an incident that occurred shortly after the initial version of my article about Alan Blinder's appointment was written in May 1994. Mr. Blinder caused an uproar by proclaiming at a Federal Reserve meeting in Jackson Hole, Wyoming, that the central bank ought to take account of the short-run trade-off between inflation and unemployment (that is, the Phillips curve) in the setting of its policy. The consensus reaction was that this attitude was inappropriate for a central banker, apparently *whether or not the points were scientifically valid*. I agree entirely with this assessment.

Guilt and Glory at the Bank of England

The past few years have been unusually eventful for the Bank of England. First, the collapse of the Bank of Credit and

Commerce International (BCCI) in 1991 raised questions about the Bank's powers and practices in financial regulation. Then Britain's withdrawal from the exchange rate mechanism (ERM) in 1992 led to the Bank's heightened influence over monetary policy, reinforced since 1993 by the quarterly issuance of the *Inflation Report* and the publication of the minutes of the monthly meetings between the chancellor of the exchequer and the governor of the Bank of England. In February 1995 came the Barings crisis, in which the venerable Barings Bank lost a fortune through speculation of its affiliate in Singapore on Japanese stock market futures. (This affair was somewhat reminiscent of the first Barings crisis in 1890 when the venerable bank lost a fortune on its investments in Argentina.) Finally, in March 1995 came a scandal that forced the resignation of the deputy governor.

In total, these events brought the Bank of England some glory and some guilt. In the case of Barings, the report of the Board of Banking Supervision, the body charged with the official inquiry into the matter, left somewhat ambiguous the possible guilt related to failures of banking supervision. More clear was the glory; by declining to step in with public funds to bail out Barings' owners, the Bank of England struck a great blow against the growth of moral hazard in the financial sector. This result—rather than the frequently cited issues of personality and who knew what when—will be the key long-term consequence of the Barings affair.

The recent economic events in Britain bring out the applicability of Charles Dickens's famous opening sentence from *A Tale of Two Cities*: "It was the best of times, it was the worst of times, it was the age of wisdom, it was the age of foolishness, it was the epoch of belief, it was the epoch of incredulity." The incredulity part refers aptly to the Bank's reaction at noon on February 24, 1995, to the announcement by Barings' directors of the extent of their likely trading losses on Japanese futures contracts. Probably the incredulity was reinforced by the knowledge that British banks are required to report promptly on risk exposures that represent 10 percent or more of a bank's capital. (This requirement does not, however, address the possible ignorance of a bank's directors about their own exposure. As possible evidence of this ignorance, Barings was recruiting M.B.A.s in London a week before the collapse with the pitch that it was at the leading edge of the derivatives market.)

Advice on how a lender of last resort should have responded to Barings' plight can be gleaned from the central banker's bible, Walter Bagehot's *Lombard Street*, written in 1873. (Interestingly, Bagehot does not use the phrase "lender of last resort," and—as an odd irony—the terminology apparently originated in the 1790s with Sir Francis Baring, the ancestor of the bank's ill-fated proprietors of the present day.) According to Bagehot, the central bank (and, specifically, the Bank of England) should lend freely in times of financial crisis on good collateral at a penalty rate. Clearly, Barings with its negative net worth—as BCCI before it—lacked the credentials for advances from the central bank.

Also noteworthy is that Bagehot did not consider central bank lending through creation of paper money—the favored vehicle now—because in his day the banking department of the Bank of England was (in accordance with Peel's Bank Act of 1844) legally separated from the issue department and its creation of notes. Moreover, Bagehot regarded as undesirable the typical hierarchical structure with a single lender of last resort at the top; he much preferred a system of similar-sized private banks, each of which maintained sizable reserves.

The Bank of England might have faced a dilemma in regard to Barings depositors, who included the queen of England, if a white knight (the Dutch company ING) had not been found with a willingness to honor all deposits in full. Under British law, the official liability is limited to 75 percent of each deposit up to a maximum payable of 15,000 pounds sterling. Since Barings catered to wealthy clients, the overall liability would have been much less than 5 percent of total deposits.

But a case could have been made that the legally uncovered depositors were worthy of protection because they had reasonably regarded their holdings with an established, apparently conservative bank as low risk. In contrast, depositors with BCCI should have perceived their high expected returns as a reward for high risk. (The two bank failures are sufficiently different that the Bank of England should not be unduly faulted for the apparent conflict with a key observation in the Bingham report, the official inquiry into the BCCI failure: "In the period since BCCI was closed [in 1991], much thought has been given to preventing recurrence of any similar event.")

Yet governments properly avoid the insurance of many private sector risks—and doubtless should avoid many more (including, in the United States, natural disasters and pension defaults). So why should governments be in the business of insuring deposits? The usual answer is the public interest in avoiding financial panics and, more specifically, protecting the payments mechanism. Arguments along these lines suggest that public insurance be limited to deposits that are backed by a small range of nearly risk-free assets. That is, the arguments favor the narrow bank, a concept that has been pushed, so far unsuccessfully, in the United States in response to the savings and loan crisis of the 1980s.

Readers will also recall the famous final line of *A Tale of Two Cities*: "It is a far, far better thing that I do than I have ever done." The Bank of England can justifiably apply this appraisal to its decision not to bail out Barings the second time around in 1995. (The Bank bailed them out the first time in 1890 when Barings lost money in Argentina.) Perhaps this noble act in 1995 will go part way to offset the increased moral hazard in international lending that resulted from the U.S.-led effort to bail out Mexico in its self-induced crisis of credit and foreign exchange. It also suggests problems in the International Monetary Fund's proposals to raise substantially the ready funds that it has available to mount Mexico-style rescue efforts. No doubt, if such a fund exists, it will also be used.

Aside

An oddity comes from the possibility of consulting with Walter Bagehot himself for advice on the Barings affair. This might seem impossible since the 1873 publication date of *Lombard Street* precedes by more than a century the recent troubles and by seventeen years the first Barings crisis. Yet the following statement by Bagehot appears in a discussion of reckless behavior by some banks: "these losses were made in a manner so reckless and foolish that one would think a child who had lent money in the City of London would have done better." To this he attached the footnote, "recent instances of amazing indiscretion on the part of great firms have been afforded by the collapse of Messrs. Baring Brothers." Presumably Bagehot would not have regarded Barings as a candidate for lender-of-last-resort treatment and would have applauded the Bank of England's decision to avoid a bailout. (The explanation for Bagehot's remarkable foresight is that the quotation comes from a 1919 edition of *Lombard Street* and refers to the 1890 affair.)

The Attractions of Price Stability

Background

I spent the 1994–1995 academic year as a visiting fellow at the Bank of England. During that period I wrote an article, "Inflation and Economic Growth," for the Bank's *Quarterly Bulletin*. One of my conclusions was that an increase in the long-term average rate of inflation by 10 percentage points per year would lower the growth rate of real GDP by 0.2 to 0.3 percent per year.

Since my article appeared in the Bank of England's official publication, it attracted a lot of attention from the British popular press. Unfortunately, the interpretation of my results was that inflation was not a big deal; the effects on growth rates looked small, and the Bank therefore ought not to worry about allowing the inflation rate to rise "temporarily." Naturally, I thought that this reaction was seriously misguided. Although the effects on growth rates seemed small, the implied costs of inflation in the long run were large. Moreover, there was nothing to gain in the short run from a following a policy that tolerated higher inflation. In order to make these points, I wrote my own article for the *Financial Times*, a revised version of which follows.

The Essay

In recent years, many central banks, including the Bank of England, have increased their emphasis on price stability. The basis for this policy is the belief that more inflation is harmful for economic activity. This belief was supported in my empirical study in the May 1995 issue of the *Bank of England Quarterly Bulletin*. I found from data for over one hundred countries from 1960 to 1990 that an increase in the average annual inflation rate by 10 percentage points reduced the long-term growth rate of real GDP by 0.2 to 0.3 percentage points. Thus, if the United Kingdom had lowered its average inflation rate between 1960 and 1990 from 7.7 percent to 2.5 percent, then its growth rate would have been higher by 0.1 to 0.15 percentage points.

These effects may seem small and may motivate some observers to call for a less restrictive monetary policy. But these inferences are wrong. Such judgments are led astray by imaginary gains from higher inflation in the short run, and they fail to appreciate the size of the losses that result in the long run from small but sustained reductions of the rate of economic growth.

In 1960, the United Kingdom was the tenth richest country in the world, with a real per capita GDP of $6,500 (in 1985 U.S. dollars and adjusted for cross-country differences in purchasing power). The subsequent growth rate of 2.1 percent per year led to a real per capita GDP of $12,600 in 1992, seventeenth in the world. If the growth rate had been higher by 1.1 percentage points, then the United Kingdom would instead have been the richest country, surpassing the U.S. level of $18,300.

Thus, a good way to think about the value of price stability is that, starting from 1960, this policy would have gone about 10 percent of the way toward the ambitious goal of making the United Kingdom the most advanced country in the world in the 1990s. If the country had adopted this policy and nine others of equal merit, then it would once again be the envy of all other nations.

The empirical evidence for adverse effects of inflation is clearest when inflation is high. For example, the inverse relation between growth and inflation is statistically significant for cases of average inflation between 15 percent and 40 percent and for those in excess of 40 percent but is not significant for values up to 15 percent. These results do not mean that inflation up to 15 percent is costless; in fact, the point estimate in this range of the adverse effect on growth is close to that in the higher ranges. A reasonable inference is therefore that an additional percentage point of inflation depresses growth in a similar way regardless of the starting level of inflation. In any event, none of the evidence suggests that more inflation in any range is favorable for economic performance. There is, in other words, no empirical support for the idea that more inflation has to be tolerated to achieve higher output and employment.

Even if 5 percent inflation is not so much worse than 2 percent inflation, there is a danger in loosening monetary policy "a little" to allow prices to rise beyond the Bank of England's target range for 1995 of 1 to 4 percent. This "temporary" lapse might allow inflation to begin its slippery slide toward rates of 10 to 15 percent or more, as in the 1970s. Inflation of this magnitude is clearly damaging, and the best way to avoid the problem is not to allow inflation to start. That is, the central bank must be eternally vigilant in its pursuit of price stability, reasonably interpreted as average inflation of around 2 percent.

Since the departure from the exchange rate mechanism in 1992, U.K. monetary policy has functioned surprisingly well to achieve low and stable inflation. A key part of this success is the increasing influence of the Bank of England, which has continually pressed for price stability as the overriding objective for monetary policy. The seriousness attached to this objective is evidenced by the quarterly issuance of the *Inflation Report* and the eventual publication of the minutes of the monthly meetings between the chancellor of the exchequer and the governor of the Bank of England.

An especially impressive aspect of U.K. monetary policy is the use of financial prices on conventional and indexed-linked bonds to infer the markets' changing expectations of inflation. The best and most objective warning sign about inflation is when yields on conventional securities rise relative to those on indexed bonds.

As an example, on May 5, 1995, the chancellor surprised the financial markets by failing to raise interest rates. The reaction of the bond markets implied that expected inflation five to ten years out had risen by seven to twelve basis points, a matter of some concern. (The consensus at the time was that the failure to raise interest rates reflected political concerns over the electoral defeats suffered by the Conservative party on the previous day.) This kind of information is available to inform policy because the Bank of England is the world leader at issuing, studying, and perfecting index-linked securities. I only wish that the U.S. Federal Reserve were as advanced in this respect. Of course, the Bank of England would do even better at monetary policy if it had more independence from the government and its immediate political concerns.

3

Fiscal and Other Macroeconomic Policies

Economic Report Cards on U.S. Presidents and U.K. Prime Ministers

Ratings of the U.S. Presidents

One popular measure of macroeconomic performance is the misery index developed by Arthur Okun, an economic adviser in the 1960s to the Johnson administration. This index adds together the unemployment and inflation rates; a higher value indicates more misery and, hence, a poorer outcome.

One shortcoming of Okun's index is that it fails to account for the starting position. Since it is difficult to generate quick changes in unemployment and inflation, it is hard to achieve a low value of measured misery if the previous administration leaves a legacy of high unemployment and inflation. A good way to correct for this effect is to consider the difference between an administration's average unemployment rate and the unemployment rate at the end of the previous term. Similarly, I look at the difference between the average inflation rate and the inflation rate during the last year of the previous term. (Since inflation is highly variable from month to month, it is better to consider the prior administration's inflation rate over its final year rather than its final month.)

Table 2
Outcomes on U.S. inflation, unemployment, interest rates, and GDP growth

Term	Inflation rate	Prior inflation rate	Unem- ployment rate	Prior unem- ployment rate	Interest rate	GDP growth rate
					2.4	
1949–52	2.3	2.7	4.4	4.0	2.8	5.8
1953–56	0.6	0.4	4.2	2.7	3.4	2.4
1957–60	2.0	2.8	5.5	4.2	3.9	1.8
1961–64	1.1	1.6	5.8	6.6	4.1	4.7
1965–68	3.1	0.9	3.9	5.0	5.6	4.4
1969–72	4.1	4.1	5.0	3.4	5.6	3.0
1973–76	8.1	3.2	6.7	5.2	6.4	1.8
1977–80	8.8	4.9	6.5	7.8	11.9	2.7
1981–84	4.9	10.6	8.6	7.2	11.2	2.4
1985–88	2.9	3.6	6.5	7.3	9.1	3.3
1989–92	4.1	4.2	6.2	5.3	7.3	1.4
1993–94	2.5	2.9	6.4	7.3	8.0	3.5

Source: Citibase data bank.
Notes: The *inflation rate* is the percentage growth rate in the consumer price index (CPI) during each term. To avoid problems with the treatment of housing costs in the data before 1985, the figures are based on the CPI exclusive of shelter. *Prior inflation* refers to the last year of the previous term. The *unemployment rate* is the average for all civilian workers over each term. *Prior unemployment* refers to the last month of the previous term. The *interest rate* is the average long-term government bond yield at the end of each term. The first value shown refers to the end of 1948. GDP growth is the percentage growth rate of real GDP during each term.

It is also useful to expand the measures of economic performance beyond unemployment and inflation, for example, to include the growth rate of real gross domestic product (GDP) and the nominal interest rate on long-term government bonds. The growth rate of real GDP enters as a shortfall from the long-run average rate for the United States of 3.1 percent per year. The long-term interest rate, a good measure of long-run inflationary expectations, appears as the change in the rate during each term.

Table 2 shows the economic outcomes for the U.S. presidential administrations from Truman's second term (1949–1952) to Clinton's first two years (1993–1994). The data reported are the average consumer-price inflation rate during the term and in the last year of the previous term, the average unemployment rate during the term and in the final month of the previous term, the nominal interest rate on long-term government bonds in December of the last year of the term, and the average growth rate of real GDP during the term.

The first four columns of table 3 show the contribution to the expanded misery index from the four underlying components: addition to inflation, addition to the unemployment rate, addition to the nominal interest rate, and the shortfall of GDP growth from 3.1 percent per year. The fifth column gives the overall change in the misery index, and the sixth shows the ranking. Rank 1, with the smallest contribution to misery, is the best.

The misery index provides a clear verdict on the worst and best of the twelve presidential terms. The two worst are the Carter administration (1977–1980) and the Nixon-Ford administration (1973–1976). These two presidencies are followed for poor results by Eisenhower's two terms (1953–1956 and 1957–1960), Nixon's first term (1969–1972), and Johnson's second term (1965–1968).

The two best administrations are Reagan I and Reagan II (1981–1984 and 1985–1988). These results are followed by Kennedy-Johnson (1961–1964), Truman's second term (1949–1952), Clinton (1993–1994), and Bush (1989–1992).

Table 3
The misery index for the U.S. presidents

President and years	(1) Change in inflation rate	(2) Change in unemployment rate	(3) Change in long-term interest rate
Truman II 1949–52	−0.4	0.4	0.3
Eisenhower I 1953–56	0.3	1.6	0.6
Eisenhower II 1957–60	−0.8	1.3	0.5
Kennedy-Johnson 1961–64	−0.5	−0.8	0.3
Johnson II 1965–68	2.2	−1.1	1.5
Nixon I 1969–72	0.0	1.6	0.0
Nixon-Ford 1973–76	4.8	1.5	0.8
Carter 1977–80	3.9	−1.3	5.5
Reagan I 1981–84	−5.7	1.4	−0.7
Reagan II 1985–88	−0.6	−0.8	−2.1
Bush 1989–92	−0.1	0.9	−1.8
Clinton 1993–94	−0.4	−0.9	0.7

Source: Table 2.
Notes: Columns 1–4 show the contribution to the misery index for each component. The inflation rate is the difference between the average for the term and the average of the last year of the previous term. The unemployment rate is the difference between the average value during the term and the value from the last month of the previous term. The interest rate

Table 3
(continued)

President and years	(4) Shortfall of GDP growth rate	(5) Change in misery index	(6) Rank (1 is best)
Truman II 1949–52	–2.7	–2.4	4
Eisenhower I 1953–56	0.7	3.2	10
Eisenhower II 1957–60	1.3	2.3	9
Kennedy-Johnson 1961–64	–1.6	–2.6	3
Johnson II 1965–68	–1.3	1.3	7
Nixon I 1969–72	0.1	1.7	8
Nixon-Ford 1973–76	1.3	8.4	11
Carter 1977–80	0.4	8.5	12
Reagan I 1981–84	0.7	–4.3	1
Reagan II 1985–88	–0.2	–3.7	2
Bush 1989–92	1.7	0.7	6
Clinton 1993–94	–0.4	–1.0	5

is the change in the long-term government bond yield during the term. The GDP growth rate is the shortfall of the rate during the term from 3.1 percent per year. The misery index in column 5 is the sum of columns 1–4 (the addition may not be exact due to rounding error). The rank in column 6 goes from lowest misery to highest misery.

The results are nonpartisan overall but cause consternation among liberals, who readily applaud the failures of Nixon and the favorable outcomes for Kennedy, Truman, and Clinton but have trouble accepting the successes of Reagan and the dismal ratings of Carter. Versions of the misery index were, in fact, generally viewed as reasonable first-order indicators of macro-economic outcomes by economists of varying political persuasions until this procedure was found in the 1980s to give Reagan the highest marks. Since Clinton scores reasonably well on the misery scale, I assume that this concept will again be widely accepted.

The use of the misery index to evaluate macroeconomic performance has been criticized on a number of grounds, one of which is that policies influence outcomes with a lag. Some empirical evidence suggests that GDP growth, unemployment, and perhaps inflation react with a lag of roughly six to eighteen months to monetary and fiscal actions. (In contrast, nominal interest rates, which are determined by bond prices, should adjust immediately to perceived shifts in policy.) I have accordingly recomputed the index to include a one-year lag for the changes in inflation and unemployment and for GDP growth. For example, the outcomes for 1950–1953 are then attributed to the Truman administration. The main conclusion from this exercise is that the allowance for a one-year lag has little effect on most of the rankings; the largest changes are that Eisenhower's second term looks better, and Johnson's second term looks worse.

Returning to table 3, for the Carter administration (1977–1980), the main sources of increased misery are the run-ups in inflation (3.9 percentage points) and long-term interest rates (5.5 points). These outcomes, related in part to the second oil crisis, reflect a complete loss of credibility in monetary policy.

For the Nixon-Ford period (1973–1976), which includes the first oil crisis, the outcomes are bad across the board but involve especially an increase in inflation (4.8 points). The poor results likely reflect the array of harmful economic policies over Nixon's two terms, including price controls (applied most aggressively to gasoline), the complete closing of the gold window, a dramatic increase in nondefense federal spending (notably for social security), the Endangered Species Act (which allowed for no weighing of costs and benefits in species preservation), and the 55–mile-per-hour speed limit.

For Reagan (1981–1988), the key elements are the reductions of inflation during the first term (5.7 points) and of long-term interest rates during the second term (2.1 points). Basically, monetary policy was reestablished as a credible force. These favorable developments with regard to nominal variables were accompanied by a recession during the early part of the first term; it is an unresolved question whether this downturn was the necessary price to pay to eliminate the high inflationary expectations that had built up through 1980. In any event, the economy grew strongly after 1982: GDP growth averaged 4.1 percent per year from 1983 to 1988, and the unemployment rate fell to 5.3 percent by the end of 1988. At the end of the 1980s, the U.S. economy was in very good shape: inflation, nominal interest rates, and unemployment had all been sharply reduced; real GDP and employment were growing strongly and steadily; and even the dreaded budget deficit had been mostly eliminated in the sense that the ratio of privately held federal debt to GDP was declining.

It is likely that the favorable outcomes during Mr. Reagan's terms were due, in part, to his tilt toward free-market policies. Mr. Reagan went some distance in lessening the intrusiveness of the federal government, notably by cutting tax rates, lowering the ratio of nondefense federal spending to GDP, and reducing the enforcement of regulations.

Free-market policies worked well in the United States in the 1980s and in other places at various times, so we apparently decided to try something else. As with the earlier move toward a defense buildup and less government intervention into the economy—which began with Carter rather than Reagan—the subsequent shift to a larger federal government started with Bush rather than Clinton. Mr. Bush raised taxes and spending, increased the minimum wage rate and unemployment insurance benefits, intensified the enforcement of regulations, and enacted an array of new intrusions in the form of the Americans with Disabilities Act, the Clean Air Act, and the "Civil Rights" Act. To his credit, however, Mr. Bush maintained a basically positive stance on free international trade, and he vetoed or moderated some proposals for increased governmental intervention, such as the Family Leave Act.

In terms of Mr. Bush's macroeconomic results, tables 2 and 3 show that the nominal variables performed well for 1989–1992, with further drops in inflation and interest rates, but unemployment rose, and the GDP growth rate was the lowest of the twelve administrations. Only during 1992, at the end of the term, did a significant recovery set in. The good parts of the results during the Bush administration can reasonably be attributed to a monetary policy that remained committed to low inflation.

Mr. Clinton's policies for 1993–1994 were similar in many respects to Mr. Bush's. Examples of antimarket policies included family leave regulation, higher marginal tax rates on the "rich," attacks on the "obscene profits" of pharmaceutical companies, increased regulatory enforcement and legislation, and threats of a trade war with Japan. These unfortunate policies were offset by positive actions on the North American Free

Trade Agreement and the General Agreement on Tariffs and Trade.

Table 3 shows that the macroeconomic results during Mr. Clinton's first two years in office were good. On the nominal side, inflation dropped by 0.4 percentage point, but long-term interest rates rose by 0.7 percentage point (through December 1994). On the real side, the unemployment rate fell by 0.9 percentage point, and GDP growth was 0.4 percentage point above the mean of 3.1. The favorable outcomes on inflation can be reasonably attributed to the maintenance of a monetary policy that was committed to price stability. On the real side, the good results for unemployment and GDP growth looked like a continuation of the recovery that began in the final year of the Bush administration.

Ratings of the U.K. Prime Ministers

During my visit to England in 1994–1995, I was struck by the unpopularity of the prime minister, John Major, and the ruling Conservative party. It was frequently stated that the country lacked the "feel-good factor." At the same time, inflation was low, and economic growth was strong. Thus, the low approval ratings seemed to be inconsistent with the economic record. To see whether this impression was accurate and to make a comparison with previous U.K. administrations, I turned to the expanded misery index, which I had already applied to the U.S. presidents.

Table 4 shows the economic outcomes during the consecutive tenure in office for the ten U.K. prime ministers since Winston Churchill's election in 1951. (The data for Clement Atlee from 1945 to 1951 are omitted; they are hard to evaluate because of their nearness to World War II.) The values shown are the average retail price inflation during the tenure of each prime minister, the average inflation in the last year of the

Table 4
Outcomes on U.K. inflation, unemployment, interest rates, and GDP growth

Prime minister and years	(1) Inflation rate	(2) Prior inflation rate	(3) Unemployment rate
Churchill 11/51–5/55	3.7	3.7	1.7
Eden 6/55–1/57	4.1	4.3	1.2
Macmillan 2/57–9/63	2.3	4.4	2.0
Douglas-Home 10/63–9/64	3.8	2.2	1.9
Wilson I 10/64–6/70	4.8	4.0	2.0
Heath 7/70–2/74	9.1	6.5	2.5
Wilson II 3/74–3/76	19.2	12.7	2.8
Callaghan 4/76–4/79	11.1	17.4	4.3
Thatcher 5/79–11/90	7.5	9.8	8.7
Major 12/90–5/95	3.1	9.3	9.2

Source: Bank of England.
Notes: The *inflation rate* is the annual percentage growth rate of the retail price index. *Prior inflation* refers to the last year of the preceding term (except for Churchill, where the value is the average inflation rate over Atlee's term from July 1945 through October 1951). The

Table 4
(continued)

Prime minister and years	(4) Prior unemployment rate	(5) Interest rate	(6) GDP growth rate
		3.8	
Churchill 11/51–5/55	1.4	4.1	3.2
Eden 6/55–1/57	1.2	4.6	1.9
Macmillan 2/57–9/63	1.9	5.4	2.9
Douglas-Home 10/63–9/64	2.2	6.0	4.1
Wilson I 10/64–6/70	1.6	9.4	2.7
Heath 7/70–2/74	2.5	13.6	2.4
Wilson II 3/74–3/76	1.9	14.0	1.6
Callaghan 4/76–4/79	4.1	10.7	3.4
Thatcher 5/79–11/90	4.1	10.7	1.8
Major 12/90–5/95	6.2	8.0	1.5

unemployment rate is the average for each period. *Prior unemployment* refers to the last month of the preceding term. The *interest rate* is the consol yield (long-term bond yield) at the end of each term. The first value shown is for October 1951. *GDP growth* is the annual percentage growth rate of real GDP during each period.

preceding minister's tenure, the average unemployment rate during the tenure, the unemployment rate at the end of the previous minister's tenure, the nominal interest rate (consol yield) at the end of the tenure, and the average growth rate of real GDP during the tenure.

One prominent observation is the increase in inflation that began in the late 1960s under Harold Wilson and expanded sharply in the 1970s under Edward Heath and Wilson again. The peak inflation of around 20 percent receded gradually through the administrations of James Callaghan, Margaret Thatcher, and Major.

The pattern for inflation is roughly matched by that of long-term nominal interest rates, which incorporate a forecast of long-run inflation. Interest rates rose sharply with Wilson in the late 1960s and continued to advance under Heath and Wilson II (to reach a peak of 17 percent in December 1974). Then rates fell under Callaghan, did not change on net under Thatcher, and fell again under Major.

For unemployment, the key observation is the increase that began in the mid-1970s under Callaghan and then continued under Thatcher (although the unemployment rate fell to 5.5 percent in early 1990). The GDP growth rate shows significant fluctuations around the mean of 2.3 percent but no clear long-term trend.

Columns 1–4 of table 5 show the contribution to misery during each prime minister's term from the change in inflation, change in the unemployment rate, change in the long-term interest rate, and the shortfall of GDP growth from its long-term average of 2.3 percent per year. Column 5, the sum of the first four columns, shows the overall contribution of each prime minister's tenure to the expanded misery index. Column 6 indicates the ranking, where the lowest number is again best.

The poorest outcomes occur during the period of rapidly rising inflation and interest rates, from the mid-1960s to the mid-1970s. The overall worst is Wilson's second tenure (1974–1976), followed by Heath (1970–1974), and Wilson's first tenure (1964–1970). Next from the bottom comes Thatcher (1979–1990), whose good results on lowering inflation are offset by the rise in unemployment and the surprising failure to reduce long-term interest rates.

The prize for best results goes to Callaghan (1976–1979), primarily because of the start of the reductions in inflation and interest rates but also because of strong performance on GDP growth. Next in the rankings is the much-abused Mr. Major (for data from December 1990 through May 1995), who gets high marks for cuts in inflation and interest rates. The third and fourth places fall to Macmillan (1957–1963) and Churchill (1951–1955), respectively.

To take account of policy lags, I again recomputed the contribution to misery when a one-year delay was assumed for the effects on inflation, unemployment, and GDP growth. The main story remains intact, although Heath is now worse than Wilson II, Callaghan's score is less favorable (but still best), and Thatcher looks a little better. (The Douglas-Home rating changes a lot, but this tenure is too brief to allow any serious inferences.)

For the present day, the bottom line is that Mr. Major's economic outcomes are strong overall in relation to those of his predecessors. In this sense, people should have felt better in 1995 than they apparently did. In any event, the experience of the United States underlines the notion that good economic outcomes are not sufficient to guarantee electoral success. George Bush's economic record was also reasonable, and he lost to Bill Clinton.

Table 5
The misery index for the U.K. prime ministers

Prime minister and years	(1) Change in inflation rate	(2) Change in unemployment rate	(3) Change in long-term interest rate
Churchill 11/51–5/55	0.0	0.3	0.3
Eden 6/55–1/57	–0.2	0.0	0.5
Macmillan 2/57–9/63	–2.1	0.1	0.8
Douglas-Home 10/63–9/64	1.6	–0.3	0.6
Wilson I 10/64–6/70	0.8	0.4	3.4
Heath 7/70–2/74	2.6	0.0	4.2
Wilson II 3/74–3/76	6.5	0.9	0.4
Callaghan 4/76–4/79	–6.3	0.2	–3.3
Thatcher 5/79–11/90	–2.3	4.6	0.0
Major 12/90–5/95	–6.2	3.0	–2.7

Source: Table 4.
Notes: The change in inflation in column 1 is the difference between columns 1 and 2 of table 4. The change in the unemployment rate in column 2 is the difference between columns 3 and 4 of table 4. The change in the interest rate in column 3 is the consol yield at the end

Table 5
(continued)

Prime minister and years	(4) Shortfall of GDP growth rate	(5) Change in misery index	(6) Rank (1is best)
Churchill 11/51–5/55	–0.9	–0.3	4
Eden 6/55–1/57	0.4	0.7	6
Macmillan 2/57–9/63	–0.6	–1.8	3
Douglas-Home 10/63–9/64	–1.8	0.1	5
Wilson I 10/64–6/70	–0.4	4.2	8
Heath 7/70–2/74	–0.1	6.7	9
Wilson II 3/74–3/76	0.7	8.5	10
Callaghan 4/76–4/79	–1.1	–10.5	1
Thatcher 5/79–11/90	0.5	2.8	7
Major 12/90–5/95	0.8	–5.1	2

of the term (column 5 of table 4) less the value at the end of the preceding term. The shortfall of GDP growth in column 4 is the difference of the value from column 6 of table 4 from the long-term average growth rate of 2.3 percent per year. The contribution to the misery index in column 5 is the sum of columns 1–4.

Economic Advisers and Economic Outcomes

Many economists (especially those who were overlooked) complained when the newly elected President Clinton chose a head of the U.S. Council of Economic Advisers, Laura Tyson, who had scant academic credentials. It is surely true that even if he limited attention to liberal Keynesians who resided within twenty miles of Harvard Square and were eagerly campaigning for the job, Mr. Clinton could have found someone with substantially more scholarly accomplishments. But it is less clear that a better economist as head of the council would generate superior policies. Moreover, if there is no gain in policy outcomes, then it is preferable to appoint a lesser light and leave the distinguished economists to continue doing the things, such as research, that caused them to become distinguished in the first place.

If we go from Leon Keyserling's term in 1949 through Laura Tyson's term, which ended in 1994, there have been fifteen chairpersons of the council. There was also a vacancy in the office for several months, mainly during the Reagan administration. The various chairpersons are shown along with their terms of office in table 6.

I have evaluated economic policy during each period by looking at the contribution to an expanded misery index, the measure that I used in the previous essay to assess presidential terms. The first column shows the change in the unemployment rate, the second the addition to the inflation rate, the third the change in a long-term interest rate, and the fourth the shortfall of the growth rate of real GDP from the average annual rate of 3.1 percent. The summation of these four values gives the contribution to misery during each term. (A larger number signifies a poorer result.)

The various council heads are ranked in the first column of table 5 in accordance with their contribution to misery. The best outcome is for Beryl Sprinkel, followed by Martin Feldstein, vacancy, Walter Heller, Alan Greenspan, Laura Tyson, Arthur Okun, and Michael Boskin. From the bottom up come Charles Schultze, Herb Stein, Paul McCracken, and Arthur Burns. The question is whether this ranking correlates positively with the council head's skill in economics. We would expect such a correlation if talent leads to proposals for better policies, if the council's proposals have influence on the policies that the government implements, and if policies matter much for economic outcomes.

I could provide my own subjective rating of each chairperson's economic expertise, but this procedure would be arbitrary (and would get me into even more trouble than usual with my colleagues). Thus, I use instead the number of times that each economist was cited in professional journals during a five-year period around the time of his or her appointment. These citation counts have been generally accepted in the natural and social sciences as good indicators of scholarly impact. I show the ranking by citations in the second column of table 7.

One immediate observation is that the list of council heads includes only one academic giant, Mr. Feldstein. Other economists with comparable or greater numbers of citations—such as Ken Arrow, Gary Becker, Milton Friedman, Robert Lucas, Paul Samuelson, George Stigler, and James Tobin—have never served as chairperson of the Council of Economic Advisers, although Mr. Tobin did have a brief stint as a junior member. After Mr. Feldstein, the citation counts of the council heads fall off rapidly, and several of these economists have either published little or—worse yet—their publications have been largely ignored in the professional journals. In this sense, Ms. Tyson

Table 6
Chairperson of U.S. council of economic advisers and economic outcomes

Council head and term	Change in inflation rate	Change in unemployment rate	Change in long-term interest rate
Keyserling 11/49–1/53	7.0	−1.9	0.6
Burns 3/53–11/56	0.3	1.4	0.5
Saulnier 12/56–1/61	−0.4	1.4	0.6
Heller 2/61–11/64	−0.5	0.1	0.2
Ackley 11/64–2/68	1.9	−1.1	1.0
Okun 2/68–1/69	0.2	−0.3	0.6
McCracken 2/69–12/71	0.6	1.3	−0.1
Stein 1/72–8/74	4.2	−0.7	1.7
Greenspan 9/74–1/77	−3.8	2.8	−0.6
Schultze 1/77–1/81	3.7	−1.1	5.0
Weidenbaum 3/81–8/82	−4.5	1.0	−0.1
Feldstein 10/82–7/84	−1.3	0.1	1.5
Sprinkel 4/85–1/89	−0.4	−0.9	−2.4
Boskin 2/89–1/93	−0.5	0.9	−1.9
Tyson 2/93–12/94	−0.7	−0.5	0.8
Vacancy 2/53, 2/81, 9/82, 7/84–4/85	−0.4	−0.7	−1.6

Table 6
(continued)

Council head and term	Shortfall of GDP growth rate	Change in misery index
Keyserling 11/49–1/53	–4.1	1.6
Burns 3/53–11/56	0.7	2.9
Saulnier 12/56–1/61	1.3	2.9
Heller 2/61–11/64	–1.6	–1.8
Ackley 11/64–2/68	–1.5	0.3
Okun 2/68–1/69	–0.8	–0.3
McCracken 2/69–12/71	1.3	3.1
Stein 1/72–8/74	0.0	5.2
Greenspan 9/74–1/77	0.7	–0.9
Schultze 1/77–1/81	0.4	8.0
Weidenbaum 3/81–8/82	3.9	0.3
Feldstein 10/82–7/84	–2.5	–2.2
Sprinkel 4/85–1/89	–0.2	–3.9
Boskin 2/89–1/93	1.7	0.2
Tyson 2/93–12/94	–0.4	–0.8
Vacancy 2/53, 2/81, 9/82, 7/84–4/85	0.6[a]	–2.1

Notes: See notes to table 3.   a. Based only on the period 7/84–4/85.

Table 7
Ranks of council heads for misery index and citation count

Misery index			Citation count[a]	
1.	Sprinkel	−3.9	Feldstein	1,642
2.	Feldstein	−2.2	Boskin	309
3.	Vacancy	−2.1	Schultze	303
4.	Heller	−1.8	Okun	161
5.	Greenspan	−0.9	Weidenbaum	159
6.	Tyson	−0.8	Heller	128
7.	Okun	−0.3	Ackley	82
8.	Boskin	0.2	Burns	75
9.	Ackley	0.3	Tyson	70
10.	Weidenbaum	0.3	Stein	43
11.	Keyserling	1.6	Keyserling	29
12.	Saulnier	2.9	McCracken	23
13.	Burns	2.9	Sprinkel	21
14.	McCracken	3.1	Greenspan	12
15.	Stein	5.2	Saulnier	7
16.	Schultze	8.0	Vacancy	0

Note: The first column is the change in the misery index, as shown in table 6.
a. *Social Sciences Citation Index.* The numbers are based only on the first-listed author of articles, are exclusive of self-citations, and have no adjustment for multiple coauthors.

is not an outlier; her citation count of seventy for 1986–1990 is undistinguished, but it exceeds that of six of her predecessors (not including vacancy) over comparable periods.

The sad conclusion from table 7 is that economic outcomes (measured by the contribution to the misery index) and the credentials of the chairperson of the council (measured by the citation count) are uncorrelated. Although some who are highly ranked on citations—such as Feldstein and Okun—do well on performance, the highly ranked Schultze ends up with the worst economic outcomes. Moreover, some of the chairpersons who are ranked relatively low on citations—notably Sprinkel, Vacancy, and Greenspan—emerge with good economic performance.

We economists can doubtless come up with numerous reasons why these results do not demonstrate that economic advisers are unimportant. For instance, although citation counts may accurately measure contributions to the advancement of a science, they may not reflect the skills that matter for effective policymaking. Moreover, the chairperson of the council—and economists more generally in the U.S. government—have rarely exerted a lot of influence over policy choices. Policies depend on political considerations, and economic outcomes are sensitive to many factors that governments do not control.

I have argued elsewhere that effective economists sometimes play a key role in economic reforms, such as in Chile, Mexico, and Argentina. It seems, in general, that economists can have a major impact, for good or ill, only when the economic problems are generally perceived as severe. In the United States, the role of the chairperson of the Council of Economic Advisers will remain extremely limited, and it is therefore a waste to have the profession's best and brightest in this position. In this sense, Mr. Clinton's selection of Ms. Tyson to head the council was just fine.

How Important Are Budget Deficits?

Budget deficits have been portrayed as a crisis in the United States for more than a decade. They were viewed as harmful throughout the 1980s during the Reagan administration, although after the end of 1982 the U.S. economy experienced sustained economic growth, low inflation, and generally falling interest rates. No matter how long it took for a recession to materialize—and it finally happened in 1990 during the Bush administration—it was inevitable that the economy's problems would be attributed to the budget deficit.

In this essay, I question the idea that budget deficits are a major crisis. The more important, ongoing issue is the scope of functions of government in terms of spending and regulations.

Trends in Public Debt

A budget deficit adds to the stock of public debt, and a good way to gauge the magnitude of this debt is to relate it to an economy's GDP. For the United States, the ratio of the privately held portion of the public debt to annual GDP fell from over 100 percent after World War II to 48 percent in 1959 and a low point of 25 percent in 1974. The ratio rose to 35 percent in 1983 because of the recessions of the mid-1970s and early 1980s, and it continued to rise because of the Reagan fiscal policy to 43 percent in 1986. The ratio fell slightly until 1989 but rose to 51 percent in 1992 because of the 1990 recession and the bailouts of financial institutions. In 1994-1995, the ratio was 53 percent.

Although U.S. budget deficits have received the bulk of media attention, the patterns in other developed countries are similar. For nine OECD (Organization for Economic Cooperation and Development) countries that I have studied in detail (Belgium, Canada, France, Germany, Italy, Japan, the Netherlands, Sweden, and the United Kingdom), the overall debt–GDP ratio in 1991 was 49 percent, about the same as that in the United States. The ratios ranged from lows of 24 percent in Germany and 27 percent in France to around 50 percent in Japan and Canada and over 100 percent in Italy and Belgium.

For many of these countries, the behavior of debt–GDP ratios since the late 1950s parallels that for the United States: falling from the late 1950s to a low point in 1973–1974, then rising until the late 1980s. Exceptions to parts of this pattern are the United Kingdom, which had a ratio above 100 percent in the late 1950s but experienced a steady decline to 32 percent in 1991; Germany and Japan, which had flat ratios of only 6 to 7 percent and 10 to 11 percent, respectively, from the late 1950s to 1974; and Italy, which had a slow increase in the ratio from 33 percent in 1959 to 38 percent in 1974.

Matching the debt figures with indicators of economic performance, such as GDP growth and inflation, reveals little association. My detailed statistical study for the ten OECD countries (the nine I mentioned plus the United States) has, in particular, shown no significant relation between the level and movement of a country's debt–GDP ratio and its real interest rate or ratio of investment to GDP. This evidence conflicts with the standard theory of the effect of public debt.

Budget Deficits and the Economy: The Textbook View

The standard theory of budget deficits, which appears in most textbooks, predicts important economic effects. If the government cuts taxes and runs a budget deficit, then households respond to the increase in disposable income partly with higher desired private saving and partly with higher consumer demand. Because desired private saving rises by only a fraction of the budget deficit, desired national saving—the sum of public and private saving—declines.

In a closed economy, accounting identities imply that national saving must equal domestic investment. Accordingly, the decline in desired national saving means that the real interest rate has to rise to reduce investment demand and raise desired private saving. This crowding out of investment in the short run corresponds in the long run to a reduced stock of capital and, hence, to lower productivity.

This standard theory implies a close association among a country's budget deficits, real interest rates, and levels of investment, but these predictions do not accord with the data. Because of this empirical failure and the increasing integration of the world economy, many economists have abandoned the framework of a closed economy to assess the effects of fiscal policy.

In an international economy with perfect markets for goods and credit, each country faces the same world real interest rate, which is determined by the world aggregates of investment demand and desired saving. Therefore, if a single country's contribution to these world aggregates is small, then that country's budget deficit has a minor influence on the real interest rate that each country faces. In the standard analysis, a deficit-financed tax cut in one country still leads to an excess of domestic investment over desired national saving in that country. But instead of raising the real interest rate, this excess of investment demand is accommodated by borrowing from abroad. That is, a budget deficit leads to a current-account deficit. Real interest rates rise only to the extent that the country is large enough to influence the global economy, or if the increase in the country's national debt induces foreign lenders to demand higher real interest payments as a risk premium.

The main new result for an open economy is therefore the much weaker tendency for a single country's budget deficit to be associated with higher real interest rates or reduced domestic investment. In contrast, if the whole world runs budget deficits, then real interest rates rise on international capital markets, and investment is crowded out in each country. These effects for the world parallel the standard ones for a single closed economy (because the world really is a closed economy).

The Ricardian Approach

An alternative theory of budget deficits relates to the research in the early nineteenth century of the great British economist David Ricardo. The Ricardian analysis begins with the proposition that if the path of government expenditures on goods, services, and transfers is unchanged, then a deficit-financed tax cut leads to an exactly offsetting increase in the present value of future taxes. The total present value of taxes cannot change unless the government changes the present value of its spending. There is no free lunch; the government must pay for its expenditures now or later, but not never.

The next step in the Ricardian argument is that consumer demand depends on the anticipated present value of taxes. That is, each person subtracts his or her share of this present value from the present value of income to determine a net wealth position, which then determines desired consumption. Since a budget deficit does not affect the present value of taxes, it must have no impact on aggregate consumer demand. Another way to express this result is that a decrease in public saving (implied by a larger budget deficit) leads to an exactly offsetting increase in desired private saving and, hence, to no change in desired national saving.

For a closed economy, desired national saving must be equated to domestic investment demand. If the Ricardian result is correct—so that a budget deficit has no effect on desired national saving—then the real interest rate does not have to change to maintain the equality between desired national saving and domestic investment demand. Hence, the Ricardian analysis predicts that a budget deficit would have no effect in a closed economy on the real interest rate or the quantity of investment.

In an open economy, the current-account balance equals the excess of desired national saving over domestic investment demand. In the Ricardian view, a budget deficit does not affect desired national saving and therefore does not affect the current-account balance. That is, budget deficits do not cause current-account deficits. There is no need to borrow from abroad because desired private saving from domestic residents rises enough to compensate for the decline in public saving.

To summarize, the Ricardian theory implies that shifts between taxes and budget deficits do not matter for the real interest rate, the quantity of investment, and the balance on current account. These conclusions are sometimes referred to as the Ricardian equivalence theorem: for a given quantity of government spending, taxes and budget deficits have equivalent effects on the economy. The effects are the same because a higher budget deficit implies an increase by an equal amount in the present value of future taxes.

Numerous theoretical objections have been raised against Ricardian equivalence, including effects that involve the finiteness of life, imperfections of private credit markets, uncertainty about who will pay future taxes, and the distorting effects from levies on income and expenditures. The last point leads to the idea that taxes (which are necessarily distorting) are best smoothed out over time. Budget deficits can sometimes be desirable—notably during wars and recessions—because they avoid the need for temporarily high tax rates at such times.

Although some of the objections to Ricardian equivalence are formally valid, they do not necessarily support the standard analysis of budget deficits. Also, the quantitative implications of these points are unclear. Therefore, the Ricardian view that budget deficits are unimportant may serve as a theoretically respectable first-order proposition. The significance of the second-order departures from Ricardian equivalence can be settled only by empirical investigation.

Empirical Evidence

The main empirical studies that test for Ricardian equivalence concern the effects of public debt and budget deficits on real interest rates, investment or saving, and the current-account balance. I provide here only a brief sketch of this evidence.

Short-term real interest rates for the ten OECD countries mentioned before turn out to be positively related to the stock of public debt but negatively related to the current budget deficit. These effects involve, however, the influence of aggregates of debt and deficits on real interest rates in each of the ten countries. The influence of an individual country's debt or deficit on its own real interest rate is unimportant. Also, the main movements in real interest rates involve nonfiscal influences, such as oil shocks, changes in the profitability of investment, and monetary policy. In addition, influences from aggregates of debt and deficits on investment in each of the ten countries have not been found to be significant. Thus, it seems that the Ricardian view may not be precisely right but also is not a bad first-order proposition. Research on these matters is ongoing.

The Ricardian idea that budget deficits would not cause current-account deficits seems to conflict with the simultaneous emergence of both deficits in the United States in the early 1980s. However, the overall evidence for the ten OECD countries reveals no significant relation between budget and current-account deficits. That is, the broad evidence is consistent with the Ricardian view that the two deficits would not be causally connected.

Conclusions

To sum up, the Ricardian approach to budget deficits amounts to the statement that the government's fiscal impact is summarized by the present value of its expenditures. Given this present value, rearrangements of the timing of taxes—as implied by budget deficits—have no first-order impact on the economy. This proposition, although in conflict with standard views of budget deficits, accords reasonably well with the empirical evidence on interest rates, investment, and current-account deficits.

It is therefore remarkable that most observers remain confident that budget deficits raise real interest rates and crowd out investment. Such confidence derives more from repetition of the story than from economic theory or empirical results.

Some Reflections on the Celebrity of Ricardian Equivalence

The idea that debt and tax finance may have identical effects on the economy, now universally referred to as Ricardian equivalence, has become familiar even to undergraduate students of macroeconomics. Such was not the case in 1974 when the *Journal of Political Economy* published my article, "Are Government Bonds Net Wealth?" which worked out the result that is now called Ricardian. Of course, I was blissfully ignorant in 1974 of Ricardo's contribution, and it took James Buchanan's comment in 1976 (also in the *Journal of Political Economy*) to give Ricardo his proper credit. Buchanan cited the discussion of public debt in the *Principles of Political Economy and Taxation* (first published in 1817), but a better treatment is in Ricardo's "Funding System," which appeared as an article in 1820 in the *Encyclopedia Britannica*.

My initial reaction to Buchanan's reference to Ricardo was that economists sometimes try too hard to read modern results into the writings of their ancestors. Moreover, I figured that it would be easy to find at least hints of the equivalence result in earlier writings, such as Adam Smith's *Wealth of Nations*. To my surprise, however, I found from a rereading of Smith that his analysis of fiscal policy was pretty garbled and surely inferior to Ricardo's. The same goes for other pre-Ricardian discussions of public debt that I examined, such as that by the French economist J. B. Say. So I eventually decided that Ricardo deserved credit for the original idea and that Ricardian equivalence was a perfectly fine terminology.

The familiarity of Ricardian equivalence today can be demonstrated by an experience that I had while working with a Boston attorney on a consulting case. I went one weekend to the lawyer's office and was met by a security guard, who asked me to sign the register. After going upstairs and working for a couple of hours, I returned to the guard's desk downstairs. He had apparently noticed my name on the register and asked, "Are you the Barro who works on Ricardian equivalence?" (It probably ruins the story to mention that the guard was a moonlighting graduate student in economics from Boston University.)

Needless to say, Ricardian equivalence is not always held in high repute by macroeconomists or the popular press. For example, Peter Passell of the *New York Times* once quoted Robert Gordon (a macroeconomist from Northwestern University) to the effect that Ricardian equivalence was an "aerie fairy theory." I was unsure exactly what this phrase meant, but I suspected that it was not complimentary, so I decided to learn more by placing the following (extra credit) question on a graduate macroeconomics exam: "The Ricardian view that budget deficits are irrelevant for the economy has been described as an 'aerie fairy' theory in the *New York*

Times. What is the Ricardian view and what does aerie fairy mean?"

Here are some of the better answers:

"I don't know what aerie fairy means. Nobody said that we would be tested on that."

"Aerie fairy could mean . . . the author learned macroeconomics when the IS-LM model [the standard Keynesian framework] was in the unquestioned ascendancy."

"Aerie fairy seems to belittle the theory as the work of an academic scribbler out of touch with the realities of saving and investment."

"Aerie fairy probably means something like I don't know what the hell you're talking about, or, I, personally, never save to pay future taxes."

"Aerie fairy means he's a Keynesian and does not like Neoclassicals."

"Aerie fairy would imply that the theory is devoid of any relevance, utterly out in space, of no bearing in the real world, and perhaps even nutty."

"Aerie fairy is essentially a meaningless pejorative term used by social commentators with leftist inclinations to dismiss sophisticated economic theories that they disagree with but cannot fully understand or refute."

"Aerie fairy means that the *New York Times* thinks this is weird and wrong."

"Just as some people believe in fairies, so might people believe in Ricardian equivalence."

"Aerie fairy means . . . totally unrealistic, wishy-washy, nonsense. No offense! Not that I agree."

"Aerie fairy means in la la land, out of touch with the indisputable, hard facts of the world."

"I don't know what aerie fairy means, but I assume it's something good."

Indexed Bonds

One of the most important things that I learned during my visit to the Bank of England in 1994–1995 was the value of issuing public debt in the form of indexed bonds. On these instruments, the nominal amounts paid as coupons and principal adjust automatically for changes in the consumer price index. Thus, holders receive a guaranteed stream of payments in real terms, and issuers face a known path of expenses in real terms.

In 1995, the U.S. Treasury was actively considering the issue of indexed bonds, and the idea apparently had a lot of support elsewhere in the government. Although this idea lacks the media appeal of some other budget-cutting proposals that were popular in 1995, it can actually deliver many billions of dollars in reduced expenditure. (An equally mundane idea—the correction of the inflation bias in the measured consumer price index—may be even more significant.)

The British experience suggests that the U.S. government would save about one percentage point on average on interest rates by issuing indexed bonds rather than standard nominal bonds. Since the privately held part of the public debt in 1995 exceeds $3 trillion, a reduction by 1 percentage point in interest rates translates into an annual saving of $30 billion in interest payments. By comparison, the elimination of the National Endowments of the Arts and Humanities and the Corporation for Public Broadcasting (all good ideas that have received considerable attention) would save roughly 2 percent as much, $650 million per year. The likely interest saving is eight times the entire 1995 budget of the commerce department (much of which would be abolished in recent proposals) and about double the budget of the agriculture department or NASA (National Aeronautics and Space Administration).

Indexed bonds have been used for a long time in countries with chronic inflation, such as Brazil and Israel. (Indexation is, in these cases, a symptom—not a cause—of high inflation.) More recently, indexed securities have become important in developed countries that are not experiencing much inflation.

They were first introduced in the United Kingdom in 1981 as part of the Thatcher government's commitment to a reduction in inflation. The Reagan administration unfortunately did not follow this lead and thereby squandered many billions of dollars in extra interest expenses. But other OECD countries have acted; indexed bonds are now issued in Canada, Sweden, Australia, Iceland, and New Zealand.

Indexed bonds have been found to be beneficial in at least four ways. First, they provide convenient instruments for institutions and individuals to use as hedges against inflation risks. The assured real rate of return in the long run is especially attractive to pension funds and insurance companies.

Second, indexed bonds provide relatively cheap financing on average for the government. The standard funding through nominal bonds tends to be more expensive because the expected real return on these bonds includes a premium to compensate for the inflation risk.

Third, the existence of indexed securities provides market signals on real interest rates, and this information can be used in conjunction with observed nominal interest rates to infer the markets' beliefs about future inflation. These data on inflationary expectations are now providing a key guideline for the formation of monetary policy in the United Kingdom.

Finally, the data on real interest rates and inflationary expectations are valuable for academic researchers. A skeptic would say that this point explains the nearly universal acclaim for indexed bonds among academics.

Governments that issue indexed bonds tend to employ long maturities: up to thirty eight years in the United Kingdom, thirty years in Canada, twenty years in Australia, and nineteen years (for zero-coupon bonds!) in Sweden. Similarly, when Britain operated under the gold standard before World War I— so that nominal bonds were effectively real bonds—the public debt was mainly long term and often took the form of perpetuities (consols), which paid a stream of coupons forever. U.S. government bonds issued before World War I were also primarily long term; for example, most of the securities outstanding in 1916 had remaining maturities in excess of twenty years.

The advantage of this long-term financing is that it insulates the government's budget from unpredictable changes in real interest rates. (The U.K. experience demonstrates that these fluctuations are large enough to worry about. Real rates on indexed bonds at a two-year horizon have varied between 2 and 5 percent since 1982.) In the extreme case of indexed perpetuities, the government knows exactly the real amount to be paid in all future periods. In contrast, with short-term debt, the need to refinance at unknown future interest rates means that the required real payments may rise or fall.

If indexed bonds are unavailable, as in the United States, then long-term funding is problematic because the unpredictability of inflation creates great uncertainty about the real value of payments far in the future. Governments typically react (reasonably if the behavior of inflation is taken as given) by shortening the maturity of their obligations. For example, in the United States, the average maturity of the public debt fell from nine years in 1946 to less than three years in 1976, then returned to about six years for 1989–1993. In 1994–1995, the Clinton administration shortened the average maturity to around five years.

The drawback of this shortening of the debt is that it makes the government's budget more sensitive to movements in real interest rates. In the extreme, the government could cut the maturity to a few months: a bills-only or floating-debt policy (which is reminiscent of Mexico's reliance on short-term Tesobonos in 1994). This policy may lower the government's expected cost of funding, but it would definitely make these costs more volatile—sensitive to each wiggle in real interest rates. Moreover, the real interest burden would typically be higher in more difficult circumstances—during recessions when inflation tends to be relatively low. (In the short run, inflation tends to be procyclical: high when the economy booms and low when it slumps. However, in a longer-run context, high inflation is a signal of bad times ahead.)

Most governments realize that an extremely short-term structure of the public debt is irresponsible—hence, except for high-inflation regimes that continue to issue nominal securities, the average maturity is kept at several years. However, it is possible to do much better than a five–year average maturity with nominal bonds. Long-term indexed debt avoids the sensitivity of real financing costs to shifts in inflation (the problem with long-term nominal bonds) and also eliminates the sensitivity to shifts in real interest rates (the problem with short-term nominal and real bonds).

Indexed bonds are a win-win proposition. The U.S. government should introduce them—preferably when inflation is not a problem—rather than waiting for the next inflation crisis.

A Program for Macroeconomic Policy

In 1991, the U.S. economy was experiencing an anemic recovery from the 1990 recession. Some common questions asked then at other times of recession were: Why is the economic recovery weaker than expected? How will the economy do over the next year? What should the government do to help? As a first approximation, the right answers to questions like these are, I don't know, I don't know, and nothing. But I find that such replies make people think either that I know little about macroeconomics or else that I am holding out on them. With respect to the first idea, I claim to be relatively well informed about macroeconomics, a position that fits comfortably with ignorance about the causes of many past business fluctuations and with considerable uncertainty about the future course of the economy. This limited knowledge not only justifies modesty about macroeconomists' ability to make forecasts but also suggests that the government should avoid efforts to fine-tune the economy. It is best for the government to provide an underlying stable framework and then mainly stay out of the way.

Because of the weak economy in 1991, some observers, including some advisers to President Bush, wanted the Federal Reserve to do more to stimulate the economy. Then, as now, macroeconomists disagreed about the role of monetary policy, notably about the effects of monetary instruments on real variables such as output, employment, and real interest rates. We know that monetary policy's main long-run effect is on nominal variables, such as the level of prices, the rate of inflation, and the level of nominal interest rates. Thus, for example, one cannot generate a permanent boom by having high or rising rates of monetary growth. In the long run, all we get from higher monetary growth is higher inflation, higher nominal interest rates, and a somewhat less productive economy.

We know for the short run that a monetary collapse, as in the Great Depression of the 1930s, contributes to declines in output and employment, and we think that unexpected monetary expansion leads for awhile to increases in output and employment. (This Phillips curve view had more popularity in the 1960s and 1970s, but it still may have some validity.) In any event, most macroeconomists agree that it is folly for the monetary authority to try to smooth out the business cycle by shifting between surprisingly high and surprisingly low rates of monetary growth. This kind of monetary instability generates confusing signals and thereby tends to worsen the functioning of the economy. Instead of attempting to fine-tune, the monetary authority's major mission should be to maintain a reliable nominal setting within which the private economy can operate efficiently. Future price levels and, hence, rates of inflation should be reasonably predictable, a pattern that in practice requires the average rate of inflation to be low.

Probably the best report card on the Federal Reserve is the level and volatility of long-term nominal interest rates. These rates reflect real interest rates and prospective inflation over the long run, but since long-term real interest rates change relatively little, the main source of fluctuations in the nominal rates is changes in the long-term prospects for inflation. Since inflation depends in the long run mainly on monetary policy, the long-term nominal interest rate reflects the bond market's view of this policy. Thus, if the Federal Reserve maintains a credible policy of long-run monetary stability, then the long-term interest rate will be low and reasonably stable.

Nominal interest rates on U.S. government bonds with ten-year maturity were low and relatively stable through the mid-1960s, but then rose along with inflation to a peak of about 7 percent in 1970–1971, an outcome that led to price controls and the closing of the gold window. Interest rates were still around 7 percent at the beginning of 1977, but the real disaster for monetary policy was the increase to around 13 percent by the end of 1980. Thus, in the late 1970s, the Fed completely lost its credibility for maintaining moderate and stable rates of inflation in the long run. The high and volatile interest rates from 1981 through 1985 can be viewed as the price paid by the Fed and the Reagan administration to restore long-term credibility. Thus, this period paved the way for the lower and much less variable long-term interest rates since 1986. Judged by the level and stability of these rates—and the correspondingly moderate and stable inflation rates—the period since 1986 merits at least an A- for monetary policy.

As with monetary policy, a good fiscal and regulatory framework provides clear-cut, stable rules that businesses and individuals can count on. Thus, if one contemplates changes in tax and regulatory policies, then it is best to consider actions that work well on an ongoing basis. From this perspective, a major deficiency of the U.S. fiscal system is its excessive taxation of income from capital. To put it another way, the government taxes saving and, hence, future consumption at too high a rate relative to present consumption.

Suppose, for example, that a corporation undertakes investment expenditures. These expenditures correspond to payments to factor inputs, workers or capital (somewhere in the economy), and these payments are subject to income taxation. Hence, the investment spending is taxed once. Later, the increased stock of business capital leads to income on capital, and the taxation of this income represents a second layer of taxation on investment.

The amount of tax on capital income depends on the manner in which investment was financed. If investment was financed by debt, then some of the capital income appears as interest payments, which are taxed in accordance with the levy on interest income. In this case, we end up with double taxation of investment—once for the initial factor incomes and later for the flow of interest income. Actually, the taxation is roughly double for long-lived capital, but the effects are mitigated for capital that is depreciated rapidly. Thus, in addition to taxing business capital too heavily, the system also favors short-lived over long-lived capital.

If investment was financed by retained earnings or new equity issue, then the capital income shows up as corporate profits, which are subject to the corporate income tax. This flow is taxed yet again when it appears as dividends (if the proceeds are paid out to shareholders) or capital gains (if the proceeds are retained). Thus, we end up with triple taxation of investment: once for the initial factor incomes, once for the corporate profits, and once for the dividends or capital gains. (The exact result depends again on the rate of depreciation.) Because the double taxation of debt-financed investment is more attractive than the triple taxation of equity-financed investment, corporations are motivated to use debt; moreover, this incentive increased with the effective rise in the capital gains tax rate in 1986. Apparently, Congress likes an environment in which it motivates corporations to rely on debt finance and Congress can then complain about the excessive reliance on debt.

Unlike macroeconomics, which has many mysteries, it is no big problem for economists to design tax systems that lessen the distortions against investment, especially long-lived investment and investment that is financed by equity. The main idea is to move toward a framework that taxes consumption instead of income. One attractive set-up allows businesses to treat investment expenditures as fully deductible current expenses; then the tax break to the corporation offsets the taxability of the factor incomes in the previous examples. In this set-up, corporate cash flow would be taxed only once and in an amount that is independent of the method of finance. For example, a corporation could pay tax on its cash flow, and no separate levies would apply on interest income, dividends, and capital gains. Alternatively, the corporate income tax could be abolished, and the taxable cash flow and tax-deductible investment expenses could be passed through directly to shareholders.

Serious proposals to implement these kinds of tax systems were made by the U.S. Treasury Department but were, unfortunately, not implemented in the 1986 tax law. If these basic alterations are unattainable, then it would be desirable to implement some less dramatic changes that lower the effective tax rate on capital income. A cut in the capital gains rate and a reintroduction of the investment tax credit are two changes of this kind.

The one caveat, however, is that these changes should be permanent features of the tax system, not additional instruments for the government to use to attempt to fine-tune the economy. This worry is especially acute for the investment tax credit, which was a favorite object of manipulation in the United States from its inception in the early 1960s until its demise in 1986. These variations in the tax credit tended to worsen the economy's performance because businesses were induced to alter the timing of investment in an effort to speculate on changes in the credit. The right policy would be to lower permanently the effective rate of taxation of capital income.

President Bush's Last Fiscal Proposals

In January 1992, President Bush gave his final State of the Union Address to the U.S. Congress. Although he had raised taxes in 1990, Mr. Bush proposed a series of tax cuts in 1992. The cuts were not enacted, but the plan has some enduring lessons because it resembles subsequent proposals, such as those offered by congressional Republicans in 1995.

Some parts of Mr. Bush's plan—cuts in tax withholding and an increase by $500 per child in personal exemptions—amount to the government's printing bonds and giving them to people. This is voodoo economics at its best, because the changes do not alter the incentives to work, produce, and invest. The only incentive effect is a stimulus to fertility, assuming that the higher child exemption is permanent.

The tax cuts would have raised the budget deficit, a minor problem because the deficit has never been very important. The one good thing that can be said about the lost government revenue is that it might have helped to restrain the overall level of spending. Otherwise the government would have taken back through future tax increases what it provided earlier through tax decreases. Since this outcome is a rational fear, one has to question President Bush's prediction that people would have spent their tax cut on "clothing, college, or to get a new car." A more prudent response would have been to hold the money until the government asked for it back later.

Other parts of the plan were more serious and addressed a key deficiency of the federal tax system: the excessive levy on income from capital. The highest tax rates, which can amount to triple taxation, apply to long-lived capital that is financed by corporate equity. From this perspective, the best type of tax reform would be a permanent cut in the tax rate on capital income.

Some of the proposals—slightly more favorable first-year depreciation allowances, lower capital gains rates, research and development (R & D) credits, and incentives for real estate investment—would have lowered the tax rate on various kinds of capital. The main shortcoming is the temporary nature of many of the suggested changes.

The proposals were dominated by the old capital–new capital syndrome. Old capital is already in place, so why waste government revenue by giving it a tax break? Target the breaks to new capital, especially to equipment and buildings that are created this year: businesses would have gotten 15 percent extra in first-year depreciation, but only if they invested between February 1, 1992, and January 1, 1993; home buyers would have gotten a 10 percent tax credit, but only if they bought in 1992 and did not already own a home (that is, only if they had no old capital). Basically, the president proposed to reward investment, but only if it occurred during the 1992 election year—not if it took place the year before or the year after. This policy is nice if one cares mainly about the level of economic activity in one particular year, but why would that be sensible?

The ultimate logic of the old capital–new capital view is that the government should enact confiscatory tax rates on existing capital to finance subsidies for new capital. The problem is that people realize that new capital soon becomes old. Investors worry about whether their capital will be taxed in the future, and they also adjust the timing of expenditures to the likely changes in government policy. If everyone knows that the government reacts to a recession with a variety of temporary investment credits—as President Bush did in his 1992 speech—then investors delay their spending until the credits arrive. This kind of speculation amplifies economic fluctuations. A much better approach, which eliminates the incentive to speculate on policy, is a commitment to permanently low tax rates on the income from capital.

Some of Mr. Bush's proposed changes—the cut in the capital gains rate and the R&D credit—can be applauded as permanent reductions in the tax rate on capital income. The capital gains tax is, however, a political lightning rod that leads immediately to debates about income distribution. What really matters for investment is the overall tax rate on the income from capital, and the capital gains rate is only one component of this overall rate. It may therefore be better to focus on less controversial ways to lower the tax rate on capital; more favorable depreciation allowances, investment tax credits, and dividend exclusions are good options if they are permanent.

President Bush demonstrated how his approach to taxation differed from his ideas about government regulation. For taxes, he first promised not to raise them and then went ahead and did it in 1990. For regulations, he first enacted a variety of new rules and then promised not to do it any more. "Read my lips, no new regulations" was a good idea—almost as good as repealing the legislation that he had previously enacted—but why would the new policy have been credible? In fact, it was not, and Mr. Bush was defeated in the 1992 election.

Infrastructure Investment and Other Public Spending

The 1992 U.S. presidential campaign seemed to reach a consensus that government spending can be valuable just because it stimulates the economy. President Bush embraced military bases, aircraft contracts, and agricultural subsidies primarily as jobs programs, and Mr. Clinton's proposed spending on transportation, communication, and environmental management seemed motivated mainly by a desire to put America back to work. If we took these notions to the extreme, then we would conclude that hurricanes and earthquakes were desirable because they increased employment in the construction industry.

The notion that useless government spending can make us better off relies on the Keynesian demand multiplier. An increase in aggregate demand due to the government's higher expenditure supposedly leads to so much utilization of underemployed labor and capital that output expands by more than the rise in government spending—that is, by a multiple greater than one. Thus, if the economy is operating at less than "full employment," then government programs are even better than a free lunch.

This extreme example of demand-side economics invites comparison with the oft-caricatured version of supply-side economics in which a general cut in tax rates leads to a sufficient rise in economic activity so that tax revenues increase. The difference is that the supply-side extreme has been observed empirically, such as in Sweden in the 1970s and Peru in the 1980s, whereas we are still waiting for the first sighting of the Keynesian demand multiplier.

The Keynesian case is often thought to be clear-cut for World War II, for which the enormous governmental outlays have been unfairly credited with getting the U.S. economy out of the Great Depression. One often overlooked fact is that the U.S. economy's growth rate from 1933 to 1941 was already the highest of any other peacetime period of this length for which information is available. Moreover, the data show that output expanded during World War II by less than the increase in military purchases. The other uses of output—private consumption, private investment, nonmilitary government purchases, and net exports—each fell to release resources for the military. Thus, the public outlays had to be justified by the value of the war effort, not by a dubious appeal to government spending as an economic stimulus. No multiplier showed up in the United States during World War II, and none has been observed in other times and places.

Since governmental programs use resources, the rationale for these programs has to come from their beneficial effects on productivity, from their direct entertainment value (as in the case of the Washington Monument, the queen of England, and perhaps the space program), or from the value that the political process assigns to the program's redistribution of income. The 1992 election campaign focused on infrastructure investment, and I shall consider what is known about the effects on productivity from this type of government spending.

A well-known article by David Aschauer in the March 1989 *Journal of Monetary Economics* noted that the turndown in U.S. productivity growth after the early 1970s coincided with a decline in the growth of public infrastructure. Subsequent research found similar patterns in other industrialized countries. Professor Aschauer's inference from this relationship was that the cutback in infrastructure spending caused the decline in productivity. The rate of return from investing in infrastructure—especially in a core group that included highways, airports, mass transit, electrical and gas facilities, and water and sewer systems—then appeared to be enormous: about 60 percent per year just in terms of the contribution to market output.

To accept this conclusion, we have to believe that the governments of various countries decided unwisely to curtail infrastructure investment and thereby reduce their country's productivity at about the same time in the early 1970s. A more plausible interpretation is that productivity and infrastructure declined in each country in response to worldwide disturbances, such as the changing mix of technologies and the movements in the prices of oil and other raw materials. Although this interpretation does not rule out a productive role for public infrastructure, it does mean that the claims for supernormal rates of return have not been substantiated. A number of ongoing research studies are trying to use these time-series data to get more reliable estimates of rates of return.

Economists have also studied the relation between infrastructure capital and productivity across the U.S. states. Richer states have more public sector capital per worker, and some investigators have incorrectly inferred from this observation that the greater amount of government capital must have caused the prosperity. More careful analyses do not find a key role for infrastructure in the determination of productivity growth across U.S. states or regions. As one example, the differences in growth performances between the Sun Belt and the Snow Belt do not relate to differences in infrastructure investment. For another, the growth rate of state per capita product from 1963 to 1986 is unrelated to the per capita amount at the start of the period of public sector infrastructure capital.

Researchers have also examined the role of public investment as a determinant of economic growth across a broad group of countries. The social rates of return to broad aggregates of public and private investment appear to be similar. Thus, the total of public investment has a positive, but not supernormal, rate of return. (In contrast, a higher level of the government's consumption expenditures is negatively related to economic growth.) William Easterly and Sergio Rebelo found in their research at the World Bank that the positive relations between public investment and growth show up mainly for spending on transport and communication, education, and urban infrastructure.

The overall evidence from the aggregate data is that investment in public infrastructure as a broad category offers reasonable but not extraordinary rates of return. This finding is consistent with cost-benefit analyses that have been applied to individual projects. The broad conclusion from these studies is that the highest returns typically apply to mundane activities, such as maintenance of existing capital (with rates of return up to 40 percent per year) and highway projects in congested urban areas (with rates of return of 10 to 20 percent per year). In other words, fixing potholes is a good idea, but bullet trains and star wars communications networks are less obvious.

Inequality

During the 1992 U.S. presidential campaign, a number of writers argued that the share of the rich in total income had grown rapidly, while that of the poor had declined. These outcomes were assumed to be bad and were usually blamed, at least implicitly, on the policies of the Reagan and Bush administrations.

Subsequent research brought out two important developments that underlay the changes in income distribution. The first, which began well before a Reagan administration even looked probable in the early 1970s, is an increase in the spread between the wages of skilled and unskilled workers. In the 1980s, for example, the wages of highly educated workers rose sharply relative to those of less educated workers. This changing wage pattern reflects technological advances, including the proliferation of computers, that make worker skill more important in the production process. In other words, economic forces are at work that governments cannot and should not seek to control. A useful government role in this area might involve improved access to education and training, not efforts to redistribute income or policies like trade protection that would retard the spread of new technologies.

The second development is a sharp increase in the share of income received by the richest individuals, an event that has even been likened to the return of the Great Gatsby. Recent research indicates that this change is tied to the Reagan period—specifically, to the tax changes in the 1981 and 1986 laws.

For the richest taxpayers, what matters is the marginal tax rate at the top; this rate was lowered on unearned income in the 1981 tax law and on earned and unearned income (other than capital gains) in the 1986 law. The response was a dramatic increase in reported income by the very rich—in nonwage income after the 1981 law and in wage and nonwage income after the 1986 law. These reactions, which have been strong enough to raise the taxes paid by the very rich, are the stuff of supply-sider dreams. But the results have somehow been taken as evidence that supply-side economics did not work. In fact, if the tax rate cuts motivated the rich to report a lot more income, then, as a matter of arithmetic, the share of income received by the rich had to rise.

The correct inference is that the cuts in the top marginal tax rates were a success and that the increases in these rates in 1990 and 1993 were a mistake. We know from experience in the relevant range that higher marginal tax rates cause the rich to report enough less income so that the taxes paid by this group decline. Soaking the rich would therefore not benefit the poor, although it would appear to improve the distribution of income by decreasing the share of reported income received by the rich.

Most researchers have relied on information about income distribution from the Congressional Budget Office (CBO), but some shortcomings in their procedures have confused matters. The CBO adjusts the underlying income data in ways that remain mysterious to outside observers, and their corrections for changes in family-size composition are indefensible. (The calculations imply that a family with a given total income is worse off if it chooses to have another child. This is like saying that a family is worse off if it buys a TV set because family income net of expenditures on TV sets is thereby reduced. Similarly, the computations assume that two single adults, who have chosen to live separately, would be better off if the government forced them to cohabit.) We can also learn more about changes in living standards from the distribution of consumer expenditure, which reflects long-run levels of income, rather than the distribution of income in a single year.

David Cutler and Lawrence Katz, economists at Harvard University, have calculated the changing distribution of consumer spending for six family types: one or two adults and zero, one, or two children. They compute for each type how much of the total pie of spending is received by the 20 percent with the least spending, the next 20 percent, and so on. For averages over the family types, the share of the lowest 20 percent in total expenditure fell from 8.3 percent in 1972–1973 to 7.9 percent in 1980 and 7.0 percent in 1988, while that of the highest 20 percent rose from 36.9 percent to 39.2 percent and 41.1 percent. Thus, in the 1980s, the share of the richest one-fifth grew by about 2 percentage points.

If we looks at income, then the poorest one-fifth appears much worse off, with only 4.6 percent of total income in 1989. In addition, the increase in the share of the highest quintile in the 1980s becomes greater—about 3 percentage points—compared with the even larger value of 4 1/2 percentage points reported by the Congressional Budget Office (CBO). Thus, in relation to the more reasonable values computed by Professors Cutler and Katz, the CBO procedures more than double the estimate of the gain by the top quintile in the 1980s. Moreover, all of the estimates agree that the movement toward a less equal distribution began in the early 1970s.

Much of the media excitement about inequality has centered on the notion that more and more of the income pie was being cornered by the extreme rich. The facts were clarified by Dan Feenberg and Jim Poterba, who studied the behavior of the 0.5 percent of taxpayers with the highest adjusted gross incomes. In 1990, this group consisted of the 564,000 tax returns with adjusted gross incomes in excess of $258,000.

Figure 6 shows the share of this rich group from 1951 to 1990 in the nation's totals of wage income and of a broader

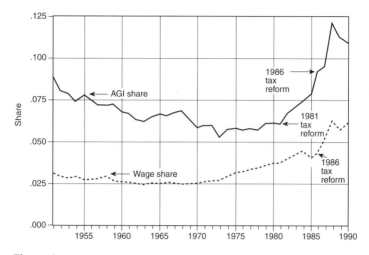

Figure 6
Shares of top 0.5 percent in adjusted gross income (AGI) and wages.
Source: Feenberg and Poterba 1993.

income measure, the aggregate of adjusted gross incomes from
the tax returns. For wages, the share rose from its low point of
2.5 percent in 1970 to 4.3 percent in 1986, jumped to 6.2 percent in 1988, and then changed little through 1990. For gross
income, the share grew from a trough of 5.3 percent in 1973 to
6.0 percent in 1981, 7.8 percent in 1985, 9.2 percent in 1986,
and 12.0 percent in 1988, before falling to 10.9 percent in 1990.

One conclusion is that the recent increase in the share of the
very rich shows up in wage income, as well as in other forms
of income, such as interest, dividends, and capital gains. The
key finding, however, is the response to changes in tax policy.

The dramatic increase in the share of wage income from
1986 to 1988 appears to be a response to the 1986 tax law,
which sharply lowered the top marginal tax rate on individual
income. The rich reported a lot more income in the form of

taxable wages, although it is not clear how the extra income divided up between reduced tax avoidance and more work. Either way, the response has to be viewed as desirable.

The share of the rich in other forms of taxable income also grew from 1985 to 1988. (The timing is complicated by the shifts of capital gain realizations from 1987 to 1986, because of the rise in the capital gains tax rate in 1987.) Similarly, the increase in the share of gross income from 1981 to 1985 reflects the cut in the top tax rate on unearned income in the 1981 law.

The strong responses of incomes reported by the rich to tax-rate changes accord with supply-side predictions and indicate that cuts in the top marginal tax rates were successful. The evidence also implies that the restoration of higher tax rates at the top, as enacted by President Clinton in 1993, would be mistakes. The higher tax rates would induce the rich to report enough less income so that the taxes paid by this group would probably fall. Although measured inequality would decline, this soaking of the rich would not benefit the poor—unless the poor would feel better simply because the rich were worse off. I presume, however, that one group's enjoyment of another group's misery is not what underlies Mr. Clinton's vision of shared sacrifices.

Soaking the Rich*

The 1993 changes in the U.S. tax law focused on increases in marginal income tax rates on the "rich." The extra revenues that were thought to derive from these higher rates underlay the administration's contention that its fiscal package was an equal mix of spending cuts and tax increases. A key issue, however, is whether the increases in marginal tax rates at the top

* Dr. Dan Feenberg of the National Bureau of Economic Research assisted with this material.

will raise any revenue at all. The history of responses to tax rate changes from 1981 to 1991 suggests that the receipts generated will probably be close to zero and may well be negative. The reason is that upper-income people are very responsive to changes in the tax code; when tax rates rise, the reported amount of taxable income drops sharply.

Neither the Democrats nor the Republicans wanted to make this argument in 1993. The Democrats, of course, did not want to acknowledge that higher tax rates on the rich would generate little revenue. The Republicans did not want to press the point because, first, they did not want to look like the advocates of the rich, and, second, if tax receipts did not rise, then they could not argue that the Democrats had raised taxes. One would have thought, however, that an increase in tax rates that produced no revenue was a good deal worse than one that generated lots of revenue.

Figure 7 shows for 1960–1991 the fraction of total federal income taxes paid by the upper 0.5 percent of the income distribution (returns with adjusted gross incomes above about $220,000 in 1991). The most relevant experience for evaluating the 1993 tax change is the period of changing tax policy from 1981 to 1991.

For the top 0.5 percent of the income distribution, the most important changes are the shifts in the marginal tax rates at high incomes. The period 1981–1991 featured a cut in the top marginal rate on unearned income from 70 percent to 50 percent in the 1981 law, a cut in the top rate on all forms of income to 28 percent in the 1986 law (except that this law raised the rate on long-term capital gains), and an increase in the top rate to 31 percent (or, more accurately, a couple of percentage points higher because of phase-out provisions for deductions) in the 1990 law.

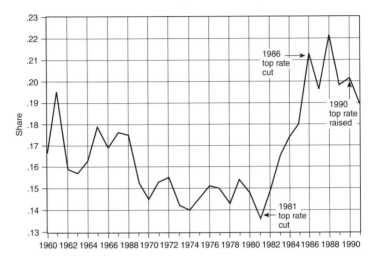

Figure 7
Share of income tax paid by top 0.5 percent of the income distribution. Source: Ibid.

The first observation from Figure 7 is that the increase in the reported taxable incomes of the rich after the 1981 law was so great that the share of taxes paid by this group rose from 14 percent in 1981 to 18 percent in 1984–1985, despite (or rather because of) the reduction in the top marginal tax rate. The much-ridiculed Laffer curve—the idea that lower tax rates could generate more revenue—worked brilliantly at upper incomes, even if not for the overall economy.

The share of the rich in taxes paid for 1986—21 percent—is inflated by the surge in capital gains realizations in anticipation of the rise in the capital gains tax rate in 1987. But the principal observation about the 1986 reform is that the share paid by this group remained nearly constant—between 20 and 22 percent—from 1986 to 1990, despite the sharp cut in the top marginal tax rate on most forms of income. In particular, in 1988, the final year of the Reagan administration—and, in that sense, the pinnacle of the "greedy 1980s"—the share of the rich reached its peak of 22 percent. (I do not know whether one-fifth is a "fair share" for the top 0.5 percent of income recipients to pay, but it does mean that the average person in this group pays forty times as much in federal income taxes as the typical person.)

More information came from the rise in the top marginal tax rate in the 1990 law. This change was followed by a *decline* in the fraction of taxes paid by the rich from 20 percent in 1990 to 19 percent in 1991. Thus, the pattern in which changes in the top tax rates cause a dramatic response in the opposite direction of reported taxable incomes works for tax rate increases as well as for tax rate decreases. This finding is especially noteworthy because the 1993 income tax changes were basically more of the same that was contained in the 1990 law.

U.S. Treasury officials claim that their estimates of large revenue gains from increased tax rates on the rich already take account of behavioral responses that lower the base of reported taxable income. This claim is misleading, because the main effects that the Treasury considers are portfolio shifts, such as the increased incentive to hold tax-exempt bonds (an effect that has to be trivial if the total supply of tax-exempt bonds does not change). Left out of these calculations are the principal shifts in reported incomes that underlie the data in Figure 7. The underlying sources of these shifts are not well understood, but they seem to involve changes in the timing of income, exploitation of tax loopholes, and alterations in work effort. In any event, the best way to project how tax payments by the rich will react to changes in tax rates is to use the information provided by the history of the responses to the 1981, 1986, and 1990 tax laws; the Treasury's estimates fail to take account of the clear message from this history.

Suppose that it is true that higher tax rates on the rich, such as in the 1993 law, will not raise revenue. Even so, the rich will suffer from the higher tax rates. The various methods employed to lower taxable income—including tax loopholes and diminished work effort—are undesirable activities that these people would have preferred to avoid. Thus, the income tax proposals will succeed in burdening the rich even if they fail to generate revenue.

(Milton Friedman made a similar point in 1962 in *Capitalism and Freedom*, p. 175: "If the yield of the present highly graduated rates is so low, so also must be their redistributive effects. This does not mean that they do no harm. On the contrary. The yield is so low partly because some of the most competent men in the country devote their energies to devising ways to keep it so low; and because many other men shape their activities with one eye on tax effects. All this is sheer waste. And what do we get for it? At most, a feeling of satisfaction on the part of some that the state is redistributing income. And even this feeling is founded on ignorance of the actual effects of the graduated tax structure, and would surely evaporate if the facts were known.")

To me it is obvious that a tax rate hike that makes one group suffer—even the rich—but provides no revenue is bad economic policy. Since I do not trust my instincts, however, I surveyed some of my left-wing friends and relatives: I asked, What do you think of a policy that makes the rich worse off but produces no revenue and therefore provides no direct benefits for the nonrich? Remarkably, the results were mixed. Some respondents would be willing to give up resources to reduce the incomes of the rich, so that some measures of income inequality would narrow. Apparently some people view the presence of wealthy people as similar to environmental pollution. One can only hope that this class-warfare mentality is not the driving force behind most policy decisions in Washington.

Retroactivity and Other Capital Levies

The 1993 budget act in the United States provided much to criticize, but an especially attractive target is the retroactive feature of the increase in the marginal tax rates at the top. People were required to pay higher taxes on incomes that they had earned before the tax change was enacted. Shifting the rules ex post facto strikes many people as unfair and illegal, even when the change applies only to the rich.

Economists view retroactivity as a form of "capital levy," that is, a tax on some previously accumulated goods (capital) or other prior activity. Capital levies are supposed to be good for incentives because the activity has already occurred: if the government raises the tax rate on last year's work, then people cannot respond by working less last year. Many policies amount to capital levies; for example, the government can default on its debt or inflate away the value of its money (after people have agreed to hold the government's obligations), renege on patents (after inventions have been made), restrict the price of pharmaceuticals (after the costs of discovery and development have been incurred), and enact rent controls (after investments in property have occurred).

Another area of policy that has analogous effects might be referred to as capital subsidies. Instead of taxing a good activity that has already happened, the government rewards a prior adverse action. For example, the government provides disaster relief payments to victims of natural disasters—that is, to people who chose to live and invest in areas that are prone to floods, hurricanes, and earthquakes. Similarly, the government invests in dams or other flood control projects after people have settled in floodplains. In another example, the government rewards past tax cheats or other criminals by enacting amnesty programs.

As with all other proposals for perpetual-motion machines or free lunches, capital levies and subsidies have their drawbacks. If the government imposes a levy today, then rational people will worry that the government will impose another in the future; that is, these policies make people worry about the security of their ownership rights. The best way to protect oneself against the threat of a capital levy is to accumulate little capital: don't save, don't invest, don't hold the government's bonds or money, and don't invent anything. In contrast, for the examples of capital subsidies, the appropriate reaction is to live in floodplains and hurricane areas and to commit crimes.

Normally, capital levies produce a lot of revenues or other benefits in the short run, but impose a burden on the economy in the long run. However, the Clinton administration managed in the 1993 tax law to design a change that contained a capital levy (retroactivity) but nevertheless raised little or no revenue. The problem is that the administration wanted a tax increase that would be paid only by the bad guys (the people who had the highest incomes—and therefore contributed the most to the economy). For this reason, the administration increased tax rates mainly at the top of the scale.

More generally, the federal individual income tax has three features that make it inefficient as a raiser of revenue. First, it has a graduated-rate structure (so that income is taxed differently depending on who gets it and when they get it); second, it attempts to tax capital income (an attempt that yields little revenue but causes substantial distortions related to saving and corporate investment); and third, it contains an array of deductions, exemptions, and credits (although some of these were

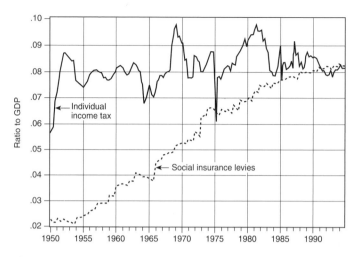

Figure 8
Income and social security taxes. Source: Citibase data bank.

eliminated by the 1986 reforms). The way to raise revenue from the income tax is to increase rates across the board or, better yet, to move toward a system that taxes labor income or consumption at a flat rate with no deductions.

To make the point directly, compare the proceeds from the complex individual income tax with those from the remarkably simple social security tax on wage earnings, a flat-rate levy on labor income with no deductions. Figure 8 shows the ratios to GDP of the two kinds of federal revenues from 1950 to 1994. (Over 90 percent of the social insurance payments in 1994 were for social security—old-age, survivors, disability, and hospital insurance—but the numbers also include amounts paid into unemployment insurance funds and government and railroad retirement plans.)

The ratio of social insurance receipts to GDP grew from about 2 percent in 1950 to over 8 percent in 1994, along with numerous increases in tax rates and in the ceiling on taxable wages. There is no appearance of a Laffer curve yet for this type of flat-rate levy; increases in tax rates succeeded admirably in generating vast amounts of revenue. In fact, since mid-1991, the federal government has gotten more from social insurance receipts than from the entire individual income tax. This achievement is notable because although social security taxes are a burden, the distortions imposed on the economy do not compare with those generated by the income tax.

The lesson for advocates of large government is that the way to pay for most of it is through a roughly uniform tax on the broad middle class. Expenditure taxes work as well as income taxes. For example, in 1991, France, Germany, Italy, and the United Kingdom each obtained revenues between 5 and 8 percent of the GDP in the form of value-added taxes (VAT)—nearly as much in relation to GDP as the U.S. federal individual income tax.

Another point, however, is that the availability of more efficient methods of taxation is not always a good idea. If the U.S. government had access to a VAT system, then government spending would no doubt be much greater than it is currently. That is, the problem with a good (efficient) tax is that it makes it too easy for the government to grow. That is why Milton Friedman said, "The only good tax is a bad tax." To paraphrase the way that my former Harvard colleague Larry Summers put it, the Republicans are against VAT because it is a money machine, and the Democrats are against it because they think that it is regressive. The VAT will be enacted, he went on to say, when the Democrats realize that it is a money machine and the Republicans realize that it is regressive. Frankly, I like Milton's point better than Larry's.

4

The Power of Economic Reasoning

The First Annual Contest for Best Monopoly in America

It's time for the first annual contest to choose the best operating monopoly in America. The finalists, selected by a panel of Harvard economists, are as follows:

1. The U.S. Postal Service
2. OPEC
3. Almost any cable TV company
4. The Ivy League universities (for administering financial aid to students)
5. The NCAA (for administering payments to student-athletes)

Some other worthy candidates, which just missed the cut, are the National Football League, the American Medical Association, and the U.S. Departments of Agriculture and Defense.

Each contestant exhibits fine monopolistic characteristics and is worthy of serious consideration for the award. The U.S. Postal Service claims to be the longest-running monopoly in America and has the distinction of having its control over first-class mail prescribed (perhaps) by the U.S. Constitution. The monopoly has preserved large flows of revenues and high wage rates despite studies that show that private companies could carry the mail more efficiently at substantially reduced cost.

On the other hand, the position of the service has been eroded by successful competition on package delivery, the entry of express delivery services, and, potentially most damaging, the introduction of fax machines and e-mail. Since these new media are bound to supplant a substantial fraction of first-class letters, the failure to get Congress to classify faxes and e-mail as first-class mail and, hence, the exclusive domain of the post office, shows a remarkable loss of political muscle. Thus, despite past glories, it is hard to be sanguine about the long-term prospects of the post office as a flourishing monopoly.

OPEC (the Organization of Petroleum Exporting Countries) was impressive in generating billions of dollars for its members from 1973 to the early 1980s. To understand the functioning of this cartel, it is important to sort out the good guys from the bad guys. The good guys, like Saudi Arabia and Kuwait, are the ones that have typically held oil production below capacity and thereby kept prices above the competitive level. The bad guys, like Libya and Iraq (when Iraq was allowed to produce oil), are the ones that have produced as much as they could and thereby kept prices low.

The good guys were responsible for the vast expansion of oil revenues during the blissful period after 1973. (Hence, these producers were responsible for the considerable difficulties endured by oil consumers.) But, unfortunately, these countries could not keep the other OPEC members in line and were also unable to exclude new producers or prevent conservation by consumers. Thus, oil prices plummeted in 1986, and only the start of the Persian Gulf crisis in summer 1990 could get prices temporarily back to a respectable level. In any event, it is unclear that OPEC qualifies for the contest: it is not really

American, and its members would probably be arrested for price fixing if they ever held an official meeting in America.

Most cable TV companies have government-issued licenses that keep competitors out. Thus, this business supports the hypothesis (offered, I think, by George Stigler) that private monopolies are not sustainable for long unless they have the weight of government behind them. The rapid escalation of prices and the limitations on services seem, however, to be getting customers and their congressional representatives progressively more annoyed. Thus, it would not be surprising if legislative action leads soon to a deterioration of the cable companies' monopoly power. It may even happen that consumers will be able to choose among cable companies in the same way that they choose currently among long-distance telephone carriers. The growing market for satellite dishes is also a concern. How will the struggling cable providers maintain a respectable cartel in this environment? This fear about the future diminishes the claim of this otherwise worthy contestant for the first annual prize.

Officials of Ivy League universities have been able to meet in semipublic forums to set rules that determine prices of admission (tuition less financial aid) as a function of applicant characteristics, especially financial resources. In some cases, the schools pooled information to agree in advance on the right price to charge to a specific customer. Airlines and other industries that wish to price discriminate can only dream about this kind of set-up.

Moreover, the universities have more or less successfully applied a high moral tone to the process: rich applicants—especially smart rich applicants—are charged more than the competitive price for schooling in order to subsidize the education of the smart poor. (It may be desirable public policy to subsidize the smart poor, but it is unclear why this subsidy should come from the smart rich rather than from taxpayers in general.)

The universities' enviable cartel position was damaged by the unenlightened Department of Justice, which argued that the price-setting meetings were a violation of antitrust laws. Since most of the universities involved agreed to stop these practices, it may be that future prices for private higher education will come closer to being competitively determined. It seems that this prospect has already motivated some distinguished universities to declare themselves as being in financial difficulty.

The final contestant, the NCAA (National Collegiate Athletic Association), has been highly successful in holding down "salaries" paid to college athletes. It would be one thing merely to collude to determine price ceilings (for example, to restrict payments so that they not exceed tuition plus room and board and some minor additional amounts), but the NCAA has also managed to monopolize all the moral arguments.

Consider a poor ghetto resident who can play basketball well but not well enough to make it to the NBA (National Basketball Association). If there were no NCAA, this player might be able legitimately to accumulate a significant amount of cash during a four-year career. But the NCAA ensures that the player will remain poor after four years and, moreover, has convinced most observers that it would be morally wrong for the college to pay the player a competitively determined wage for his or her services. For many economists, this interference with competition—in a setting that has no obvious reasons for market failure—is itself morally repugnant. But the outrage is compounded here because the transfer is from poor ghetto residents to rich colleges. Compare the situation of contestant number 4, the Ivy League universities, in which the transfer from rich to poor students can readily be supported on Robin Hood grounds.

The NCAA has the much more difficult task of defending a policy that prevents many poor individuals from earning money. Incredibly, this defense has been so successful that it has even allowed the organization to maintain the moral high ground. When the NCAA maintains its cartel by punishing schools that violate the rules (by paying too much), almost no one doubts that the evil entities are the schools or persons who paid the athletes rather than the cartel enforcers who prevented the athletes from getting paid. Given this extraordinary balancing act, the decision of the panelists was straightforward: the NCAA is the clear and deserving winner of the first annual prize for Best Monopoly in America.

The panel of economists also considered briefly an award for the least efficient monopoly in America. This choice was easy. It goes to the American Economic Association, which has been a dismal failure at establishing licensing requirements or other restrictions on entry into the economics profession. It is a sad state of affairs when almost anyone can assume the title of economist.

This Tax Amnesty Will Work Only Once*

Every now and then some state or city government carries out an amnesty in which past tax evaders are forgiven fines and criminal punishments if they come forward and pay what they owe. These programs surely generate extra revenue in the short run, but this attraction is offset by people's expectations that new amnesties might occur later. These expectations lower the penalties that people anticipate for future tax evasions and thereby reduce the government's tax receipts later. To counter

---

* Professor Alan Stockman assisted with this material.

these beliefs, governments typically announce that the amnesty is a one-time happening; in fact, they usually combine the amnesty with a promise of tighter enforcement and penalties for future offenses.

Why would anyone believe these announcements? After all, if an amnesty generated a lot of revenue once and was therefore attractive to politicians, why would it not prove to be attractive again in the future? Then it is reasonable for people to believe that tax amnesties will recur from time to time, and hence that the penalties for evading taxes will be less than they used to be. This means that amnesties would generate a lot of money when they were in effect—at which times they would be applauded as successes by politicians and some of the media—but would lower tax collections at other times (and probably reduce the overall take). But since it would be hard to prove that the later reductions had anything to do with the amnesties, the popularity of these programs might remain intact.

The general problem is a familiar one to economists and, in fact, fills a whole literature (referred to as time-inconsistency problems of government policy). For example, it is appealing to abolish patents on pharmaceuticals or other inventions in order to increase competition, but the expectation of future abolitions deters people from inventing things. Similarly, it looks attractive to tax old investments more harshly than new investments, except that people are smart enough to figure out that new things eventually become old. Or again, it may look great to default on public debt (perhaps through surprise inflation), as long as debt holders do not realize that the government's new obligations will later be old ones.

Clearly a tax-amnesty program will be most successful if the government can somehow convince people that it would never effect another amnesty in the future. Since simple promises would carry no weight, the following plan is suggested. First, announce that a tax amnesty will be in effect for the next year. Then, after the amnesty ends, the government should announce that it was only kidding. All those who came forward with past tax offenses will be punished as though the amnesty had not existed. This proposal has the following advantages. First, it collects a lot of revenue from those who respond to the amnesty. Second, it avoids the moral dilemma of allowing criminals to escape punishment. Third, it has no adverse consequences for future tax collections because people have no reason to think that amnesties would recur. In fact—as is desirable here—the government would have no way ever to convince people that a future amnesty was for real.

Now some people may object that the failure to follow through on the amnesty is dishonorable. But this reasoning is backward. It is the amnesty itself that proposes to ignore the rules for awhile. Reneging on the amnesty is merely a reconfirmation that the government would stick to its rules. Thus, by reneging, the government encourages people to take rules seriously, whereas by following through, the government might make people doubt all sorts of rules.

The only problem with this plan—which describes a sting operation that could be applied to crimes more serious than tax evasion—is that, in phase I, the tax cheaters must be unaware that phase II entails reneging on the amnesty. Probably this plan would have worked better if it had not been published.

School Choice

School choice programs that include private schools are a promising way to deliver improved education, especially for children from poor families. Experiments such as Milwaukee's have shown some success, but systems that include any funding for private schools in the United States are rare. Not coincidentally, in 1990, only 12 percent of elementary and secondary students attended private schools, with 12 percent of the private enrollment in nonsectarian institutions (8 percent at the primary level and 14 percent at the secondary level). Catholic schools were the dominant private provider, with about 70 percent of overall private enrollment.

The overwhelming choice of public over private education does not mean that most people view public schooling as superior. Various studies, notably those by James Coleman and his associates, have found that students with a given level of native ability do better when they attend private institutions, especially Catholic schools in inner cities. The key element that sustains the dominant position of public schools is that individual consumers regard the public option as free and the private one as expensive; Catholic schools are able to thrive in spite of this obstacle because church subsidies maintain low levels of tuition. Nonsectarian schools, including the elite places such as Andover and St. Paul's, typically have to rely on high levels of tuition with limited amounts of financial aid and therefore can serve only a small, privileged minority.

The central element of school choice plans is the use of vouchers or tax credits to level the playing field between public and private schools. The demand for private schools would expand accordingly, and the increased incidence of private education would be expected to improve the average performance of graduates. The most dramatic change would be predicted for poor families, who typically lack access at present to private schools or high-quality public schools.

A substantial part of the opposition to school choice plans, such as the proposal rejected in 1993 in California, comes from two groups: well-off suburbanites and public school employees. Suburbanites are usually at least somewhat satisfied with their local public schools and do not wish to incur higher taxes to give money to people who already use private schools. Public school teachers and other employees do not want to lose an entrenched position that ensures a reasonable income even when performance is bad. For these opposition groups, a key concern is how a school choice plan and the consequent expansion of private alternatives would affect the public schools. Would the quality and levels of funding diminish, or would the increased competition force the public schools to do better?

Research by Caroline Hoxby in her Ph.D. dissertation at MIT ("Do Private Schools Provide Competition for Public Schools?") provides evidence on this issue. The main information comes from the interaction between an area's usage of private schools, especially Catholic schools, and measures of the quality of public education. The information in these data is better than that provided by existing school choice programs because it is hard to discern long-run responses to experiments, such as the one in Milwaukee, that are relatively new and are plausibly perceived as temporary by potential students and schools. Moreover, existing school choice plans tend to contain serious restrictions on the options of schools and students.

The key challenge is to isolate the effect of greater availability of private schools on the performance of the public schools. This work is a challenge because the simple relation between an area's private school use and the quality of the public schools could, in theory, be positive or negative.

First, if an area's public schools are performing badly, then more families would be motivated to use private schools. This response tends to generate a negative relation between public school quality and private school use. Second, if an area's families are wealthier and better educated, then private school use and public school quality are both likely to be higher. This interaction tends to generate a positive relation between public school quality and private school use. Finally, an increased availability of private schools provides competition that motivates the public schools to perform more efficiently. The implied positive relation between private school use and public school quality is the one that we would like to measure if it exists.

The Hoxby study isolates the relation of interest by seeing how cross-county differences in the costs of providing private education affect the quality of the public schools. In practice, the U.S. experience dictates a reliance on information about sectarian private schooling. The cost differences for operating these sectarian schools come from variations across counties in the population density of Catholics or of other religious denominations—Lutheran, Jewish, and Episcopalian—that run significant numbers of private schools.

The key conclusion is that greater use of private schools, driven by differences in costs, leads to improved performance of public school students and to greater per-pupil spending in the public schools. These results hold when one holds constant an array of individual and county characteristics, including levels of income and parental education and a person's religion and race.

One finding is that an increase by 10 percentage points in the share of a county's enrollment in private secondary schools is estimated to raise by 0.3 years the highest grade completed by the average public school student by age twenty-four. This increase in the share of private enrollment is also estimated to raise a public-school student's probability of receiving a high school diploma by age nineteen by 2 percent and to increase the wage earned by the average public school student at age twenty-four by 5 percent (partly because the student is more likely to move to a more prosperous area and partly because the student's position in the earnings distribution improves). Thus, the presence of the private alternatives means that the students who remain in the public schools achieve at higher levels.

The data also show that governments respond to greater competition from private schools by raising teachers' salaries and overall spending per pupil in the public schools. An increase by 10 percentage points in the share of a county's enrollment in private secondary schools is estimated to raise the starting salary for a teacher with a B.A. in public secondary schools by $460 and to raise per-pupil spending in these schools by $340 (all measured in 1980 dollars).

In terms of the groups that typically oppose school-choice plans, the Hoxby evidence implies that the public school teachers who retain their positions—presumably the most qualified teachers—ought to be happy when private schools become more available. However, the less-qualified public school teachers are likely to be harmed. For wealthy suburbanites who use public schools, the improvement in school quality would provide a benefit. However, these suburbanites would likely face higher tax bills.

If we combine the Hoxby evidence with previous results on the performance of private schools, then the inference is that full school choice programs would improve student achievement whether the students shift to private schools or stay in the public system. In other words, school choice is a good idea, especially for less-well-off groups that now lack access to quality education.

Privatization American Style

Privatization has been a central issue in the formerly socialist countries and has also been important in Western Europe, Latin America, and elsewhere. The United States has participated little in this activity because the U.S. government has fortunately never had much ownership of the means of production (aside from the post office, Tennessee Valley Authority, oil reserves, a few railroads and airports, and a lot of buildings and military hardware). Contractions of the U.S. public sector might be a good idea, but they would look more like reduced transfers and regulations rather than privatization.

Congressional Republicans have been pushing to return a lot of power and spending authority from the federal government to states and localities, and these lower levels of government have also been the focus of privatization in the United States. In the long run, the key area will be the shift of education from public to private provision, probably financed by taxes through school choice programs. But up to now, the main movement has been at the city and county level and has involved primarily the shift of services from direct public provision to contracting out with private providers. These actions reduce government spending to the extent that the farmed-out services are less costly.

Table 8 shows the fraction of services privatized—that is, contracted out rather than provided directly by county government—in 1987 and 1992 in twelve activities that range from hospitals and libraries to public transit and utilities. The underlying information comes from the 1987 and 1992 Censuses of Governments, as reported in "Privatization in the United States," by Professors Lopez-de-Silanes, Shleifer, and Vishny (henceforth referred to as the LSV study). The table shows that

Table 8
Privatization fractions for county services

Type of service	1987	1992
Hospitals	0.34	0.46
Landfills	0.20	0.26
Libraries	0.14	0.23
Nursing homes	0.24	0.28
Public transit	0.37	0.48
Sewerage	0.18	0.30
Stadiums	0.21	0.29
Fire protection	0.22	0.37
Airports	0.30	0.36
Water supply	0.21	0.35
Electric utility	0.74	0.96
Gas utility	0.78	0.89
Total, 12 categories	0.24	0.34

Source: Lopez-de-Silanes, Shleifer, and Vishny, 1995.
Notes: The numbers show the fraction of services contracted out rather than provided directly by county government for the 3,042 U.S. counties. The figures do not consider nonprovision (which occurs most often when services are provided by municipalities rather than counties) or less common methods of privatization, such as volunteerism, franchising, vouchers, and service shedding (elimination of the designated activity as a governmental function). The source is table 1 of the LSV study, which is described in the text.

the privatized share of the twelve activities rose overall from 24 percent in 1987 to 34 percent in 1992. Most of this privatization did not result from switches in mode of provision for existing activities but rather from a dramatic movement toward the private option in services that were newly provided by county governments. (Rubbish collection, one of the most privatized areas, and street maintenance are missing from the table because they were not covered by the 1987 census.)

The LSV study notes that contracting out remains a minority choice of local government, although many studies have shown that this method usually reduces costs substantially without compromising the quality of service. To explain this behavior, the study views the public-versus-private choice as emerging from a political equilibrium in which politicians receive patronage-style benefits from direct government operation, public sector unions gain from higher wages and employment under public provision, and this unholy alliance between politicians and unions is constrained by voters' concerns about taxes. Thus, the prediction is that privatization will be more likely if the legal system limits the amount that public officials can gain from patronage, if public employee unions are more restricted, and if local spending and borrowing authority are more constrained. The findings are of particular interest because the factors explored—such as restrictions on local government debt and deficits, limitations on union power, and avoidance of state government bailouts—resemble parts of the Republican agenda for the federal government.

Table 9, taken from the LSV study, shows how various factors influence the probability that the twelve kinds of services will be privatized (contracted out, rather than provided directly by county government). Two state laws that limit the potential for patronage—a requirement to use a merit system in hiring and the imposition of purchasing standards—stimulate privatization. If both laws are in effect, then the probability of the private option is increased by 13 percentage points.

Two legal restrictions on the power of public sector unions—the exclusion of political activity by government employees and the prohibition of strikes by public workers—raise the likelihood of privatization. The two rules together raise the probability of privatization by 18 percentage points. A less important but

Table 9
Estimated effects on the probability of privatization

Variable	Estimated effect
Laws that influence political patronage	
State law requires merit system for county hiring	.026
State law sets local purchasing standards for county spending	.103
Laws and activities involving public employees and unions	
State law prohibits political activity by public employees	.065
State law forbids strikes by public employees	.110
Fraction of county government workers not in unions rises by ten percentage points	.008
Laws that affect county government budget constraints	
State law prevents county from borrowing short term	.044
State law imposes debt limits on counties	.063
State law mandates balanced budget for counties	−.058
State law does not provide for state takeover of local finances	.098
A measure of political ideology	
County vote for Republican candidate in nearest gubernatorial election rises by ten percentage points	.011

Source: Ibid.
Note: The coefficients show the estimated effect of each variable on the probability that a public service will be contracted-out rather than provided directly by a county government.

supporting effect is that the incidence of private provision increases with the fraction of public employees who are not unionized. The probability of privatization rises by 1 percentage point if the unionization fraction falls by 10 percentage points.

Privatization is also more likely if state laws make county budget constraints tighter. The rules that stimulate private provision are the prohibition of county short-term borrowing, the imposition of debt limits at the county level, and the preclusion of state-level bailouts through takeovers of county finances. (The last provision is the state-local analogue to the elimination of the potential for bailouts of troubled countries like Mexico by the International Monetary Fund and the U.S. government.) The combination of these three budget constraint rules raises the probability of privatization by 20 percentage points.

Surprisingly, however, a state-mandated balanced budget at the county level has the opposite effect: it lowers the probability of private provision by 6 percentage points. Possibly this pattern arises because a mandate for the submission of a balanced budget is an indicator that serious methods for restricting spending are not being employed. Since the balanced budget method of curtailing government is currently favored by Republicans at the federal level, these results at the local level would argue for a shift in approach.

Finally, the LSV study considers whether purely ideological factors—represented here by the fraction of a county's Republican vote in the nearest gubernatorial election—matter for privatization. The result is that 10 percentage points more of Republican vote raise the chance of privatization by 1 percentage point. Thus, ideology matters a little, but not nearly as much as the legal provisions that have already been discussed.

If we interpret privatization of local activities as less (or perhaps better) government, then the LSV study has some important lessons for legal changes that would generate a downsizing (or improvement) of the public sector. Good ideas include a civil service system with merit provisions, required purchasing standards, limitations on the power and extent of public employee unions, and rules that limit the ability of government to borrow and spend. However, some of these rules—prohibition of short-term borrowing, debt limits, and preclusion of bailouts from higher levels of government—work better than balanced-budget requirements.

Second-Hand Smoke

I admit that I dislike cigarette smoke. I also do not understand why apparently reasonable people, including a few famous economists, voluntarily expose themselves to the hazards and general unpleasantness of smoking. But I recognize these tastes as my own and would never propose to use the government to get smokers to "do the right thing."

Many people, including some U.S. government officials, are more eager for the government to intervene to reduce cigarette consumption. Flushed, apparently, with our brilliant successes in the control of illicit drugs—such as marijuana, cocaine, and heroin—the head of the FDA (Food and Drug Administration) would like to classify cigarettes as drugs. Presumably the idea is that cigarettes could eventually be prescribed only for medicinal purposes; since there are none, the long-run aim must be prohibition.

The experience with drug enforcement shows that prohibitions of recreational drugs drive up prices, stimulate illegal activity, have only a moderate negative effect on consumption, and impose unacceptable costs in terms of high crime, expansion of prison populations, and deterioration of relations with the foreign countries that supply the outlawed products. A better idea would be to leave intact the existing regulatory structure for cigarettes—which includes substantial but not outrageous tax rates and restrictions on sales to minors—and apply this apparatus to the currently illegal drugs.

Although smoking has been demonstrated to harm smokers, the regulation of this activity still runs into the traditional libertarian objection that well-informed persons ought to be allowed to assume these risks if they wish. (The familiarity of this point does not make it less compelling.) Thus, advocates of increased regulation have found it important to argue that smoking also injures "innocent parties," notably through second-hand smoke. The Environmental Protection Agency (EPA), relying mainly on evidence from nonsmoking spouses of smokers, reported in 1993 that second-hand smoke is a serious health hazard.

Even if these hazards exist—and the medical evidence on this point is seriously in doubt—the case for government regulation would remain incomplete. In a restaurant, for example, the owner can determine whether to make the premises nonsmoking or to have nonsmoking sections. This decision will be guided—if the owner is a greedy maximizer of profit—by a weighing of the benefits from a smoke-free environment to nonsmokers (expressed in terms of their willingness to pay and to patronize the restaurant) against the costs to smokers (expressed again in terms of their demand for the restaurant's services). The restaurant will be smoke free if the gains to nonsmokers—including the value of reduced medical risks—exceed the costs to smokers. One would also expect some restaurants to cater to smokers and some to nonsmokers.

The same argument holds for airplanes, employers, commercial buildings, and so on. It also applies to the interactions among spouses; even if a smoker damages the health of his or her nonsmoking spouse, the pair does not need the assistance of the government to decide whether smoking should occur in the household (or, indeed, whether they should be married).

The relations between smoking parents and (nonsmoking) children are more complex. Parents typically care about their children and thereby take account of the effects of their actions on the children's welfare. A smoker has therefore determined that his or her direct benefit is more important than the cost imposed on the children. (The main cost is probably not from second-hand smoke but rather the increase in the probability that the child will subsequently become a smoker.) Unlike a spouse, however, the child is not a voluntary, well-informed participant in a contract and would be unable to express an aversion to the parent's smoking in terms of some kind of future promise to pay.

The government has, accordingly, often prevented parents from making unrestricted decisions on matters that affect their children's welfare, as in laws on compulsory schooling and work hours. Since most parents are better equipped and motivated than the government to consider their children's well-being, it is unclear that this type of regulation has net social benefits. In any case, an extension of this reasoning could be used to rationalize restrictions on parental smoking in the home. I suppose that these restrictions could be administered by an EPA police force.

Despite assertions by the EPA, the statistical evidence for health risks from second-hand smoke is extremely weak, even by the standards of an empirical economist. The evidence comes primarily from epidemiologic studies, most of which rely on the experience of nonsmoking spouses of smokers. The research studies available through 1989 were carefully evaluated in an international symposium at McGill University and published in a volume edited by Ecobichan and Wu as *Environmental Tobacco Smoke*. With respect to lung cancer, the conclusion was, "The weak and inconsistent associations seen in the epidemiologic studies of ETS [environmental tobacco smoke] and lung cancer, the fact that bias and confounding cannot be ruled out, and questions about the reliability of the reported results, all indicate that these data do not support a judgment of a causal relationship between exposure to ETS and lung cancer" (p. 111).

The difficulties in establishing a link between ETS and lung cancer are illustrated in a recent study (*American Journal of Public Health*, November 1992) that included a relatively large sample of 618 nonsmoking or ex-smoking white Missouri women who were diagnosed with lung cancer between 1986 and 1991. The authors report no overall effect from the presence of a smoking spouse on the probability of contracting lung cancer. They found, however, that the spouse of someone who smokes at low or moderate levels has a 30 percent *lower* probability of lung cancer than the spouse of a nonsmoker, whereas the spouse of someone who smokes at a high level has a 30 percent higher probability. The authors choose to emphasize the last result, but the findings as a whole make no sense in terms of a causal relation. Remarkably, the conclusion was that "comprehensive actions to limit smoking in public places and worksites are well-advised." Such judgments, like those of the EPA, must come from prior beliefs rather than from the scientific results.

The difficulties with the 1992 Missouri study typify the problems in this field; the shortcomings stressed in *Environmental Tobacco Smoke* are a greater tendency to publish results that show significant and harmful effects of ETS, the tendency for nonsmokers to misreport their status (combined with the likelihood that spouses of smokers will be smokers), and the failure to take account of socioeconomic characteristics that are correlated with health outcomes and with smoking status.

Large effects from second-hand smoke on health outcomes are implausible, in any case, because the exposure levels are too low. According to *Environmental Tobacco Smoke* (p. 229), active smokers receive one hundred to one thousand times the nicotine of persons exposed to ETS. Nicotine is not like cyanide, for which small doses can be lethal; even in active smokers, the adverse effects take many years to materialize. Thus, it is implausible that doses of 1/100 or 1/1000 of those experienced by active smokers would have any noticeable health impact, such as that claimed by the EPA.

A connection between parental smoking and children's health has more foundation; for example, *Environmental Tobacco Smoke* notes, "There is better evidence that exposure to tobacco smoke has some effect on the respiratory health of children than in other areas" (p. 227). Interestingly, however, the effect is detectable only in young children; the link between health outcomes and parental smoking seems to disappear once children are older than two years old. A possible explanation is that smoking by the mother during pregnancy, rather than sec-ond-hand smoke, is the main culprit.

Another approach would focus on the well-documented harmful effects of smoking on smokers. The case for government intervention could then come from paternalism; the government knows better than ignorant individuals about what makes them better off. A superficially more compelling argument is that a person's health is everybody's business because society pays for at least a portion of most people's health care. (One of the problems with socialized medicine is that this linkage becomes stronger.) This point has been used to justify mandatory use of seat belts in cars and of helmets on motorcyclists. The argument is dubious in those areas but is particularly suspect for smokers, who tend to have relatively brief terminal illnesses—at least from lung can-cer—and often die before they collect much in retirement bene-fits from social security. From this perspective, the usual economic analysis would argue for a subsidy to smoking.

The case for harmful effects on innocent parties is stronger for alcohol than for cigarettes; for example, drunk driving is a serious problem that has not been satisfactorily handled by courts or insurance companies. The only reason that we are now increasing restrictions on tobacco, rather than alcohol, is that we already tried it once for alcohol, and it worked badly. There is no reason to expect better results for cigarettes.

The final recourse is to admit that the scientific evidence on the health hazards of second-hand smoke is flimsy, but to point out—correctly—that this evidence also does not conclusively rule out a small effect. Why not then err on the side of safety and restrict people's exposure to second-hand smoke? One problem with this logic is that it applies to a virtually unlimited array of activities, starting with global warming and depletion of the ozone layer. We would be in serious trouble if we spent liberally and took restrictive actions in every area in which a semirespectable theory of health risk had been advanced but had not been shown scientifically to be significant. In no time at all, imaginative environmentalists would exhaust the entire gross national product on activities with low or negative social rates of return.

Epilogue

Shortly after writing the original version of this essay for the *Wall Street Journal*, I received a comment from a friend. He said that he was the only one of his circle of doctors who believed that I had not been bought out by the tobacco industry. Then a little while later I received a proposal from a tobacco company, RJR Nabisco, to include the column (uncensored) in its advertising campaign for smokers' rights in various newspapers and magazines.

This offer presented a dilemma. On the one hand, since I regarded the article as accurate, why should I decline this sort of publicity? On the other hand, the dissemination of the material in this format would undoubtedly convince more people that I was merely a spokesman for the tobacco industry—indeed, a paid spokesman should I accept the offered honorarium. Another consideration was that I personally dislike smoking. On the other hand, I do not regard tobacco companies or their employees as particularly evil or angelic, and I would probably have accepted the fee and publicity under similar circumstances from a firm in another industry.

I consulted a liberal colleague for advice, sure that I would be counseled to avoid association with a nasty tobacco company. But no, the advice was that it all depended on the size of the fee. Since my heart was pure, I should go ahead as long as the fee was large enough; otherwise the accompanying flak would not be worth the trouble. So I followed this counsel. The fee was not that big in relation to the likely trouble, and I declined RJR Nabisco's offer. (I also rejected a later proposal from Philip Morris to include the column in its publicity material.) Most people seem to think that I made the correct and honorable decision (although they usually disagree with the stress on the size of the fee). I still think, though, that the more courageous course would have been to allow the tobacco companies to use the material as they wished.

How Much Is an Endangered Species Worth?

The U.S. Endangered Species Act of 1973 contains little that an economist would love. As Richard Stroup of the Political Economy Research Center puts it, the act "allows the U.S. Fish and Wildlife Service (FWS) to ignore the constraint of scarcity, giving them the power to simply order other agencies and private landowners to do what the FWS biologists say must be done to help the listed species survive." In the process, the FWS is allowed to take control of private land without compensation, a straightforward violation of the takings clause of the Fifth Amendment. (The FWS contends that it does not assume ownership of the private land; it merely tells the owner how to use it. This argument may work in court if the judge has never taken a course in principles of economics.)

In 1978, Congress allowed some relief from the unbending provisions of the act by creating the Endangered Species Committee. This committee can weigh costs and benefits by exempting a federal agency's action from the act's provisions if "the benefits of such action clearly outweigh the benefits of alternative courses of action consistent with conserving the species on its critical habitat."* In practice, the granting of exemptions has been rare—for example, to allow a small amount of logging in the environment of the spotted owl on federal lands in the Pacific Northwest.

Private individuals are, in any event, ineligible to apply for relief from the Endangered Species Act, no matter what the costs. For example, in the case of the kangaroo rat, Richard Stroup observes, "The October, 1993 fires in Riverside County, California destroyed many homes. Firebreaks, which normally clear a path in the brush to interrupt the spread of fires, had been prohibited for 1993 by the FWS in order to protect the habitat of the kangaroo rat, a listed species. Ironically, the intense fires probably destroyed the rats living there also. No compensation was paid by the FWS to the homeowners for their losses." No doubt we are all comforted by assurances from the GAO (General Accounting Office) and Congressman Gerry Studds that the FWS restrictions bore no responsibility for the fire damage.

Although the FWS may pretend that all endangered species are equal and are all worth an infinite amount of resources, the

---

* Endangered Species Act Amendments of 1978, public law 95-632.

Table 10
Top-ten list of endangered species by total spending (1989–1991)

Common name	Spending ($ million)
1. Bald eagle	31.3
2. Northern spotted owl	26.4
3. Florida scrub jay	19.9
4. West Indian manatee	17.3
5. Red-cockaded woodpecker	15.1
6. Florida panther	13.6
7. Grizzly (or brown) bear	12.6
8. Least Bell's vireo	12.5
9. American peregrine falcon	11.6
10. Whooping Crane	10.8

Source: Metrick and Weitzman, 1995

Service and other government agencies actually make choices about how to allocate limited funds among the candidates. Since 1988, Congress has required the FWS to provide "an accounting on a species by species basis of all reasonably identifiable federal [and some state government] expenditures for the conservation of endangered or threatened species."* The spending figures exclude amounts that cannot be assigned to individual species and do not include the often far greater costs imposed on the private sector or other government agencies. Nevertheless, the numbers provide information about the priorities that the government assigns to the protection of different animals.

Andrew Metrick and Martin Weitzman, in "Patterns of Behavior in Endangered Species Preservation," have tried to infer the priority system that underlies the government's spending decisions. They begin with table 10, which shows the top ten

---

* Endangered Species Act Amendments of 1988, public law 100-478.

animals by total expenditures from 1989 to 1991. Remarkably, these ten account for 54 percent of the overall spending on the 554 species or subspecies that were officially listed as endangered or threatened in November 1990. Thus, the government is highly selective about which creatures to favor.

Professors Metrick and Weitzman comment about the curious composition of the favored ten:

The species . . . are all mammals or birds . . . mostly relatively large mammals or birds. Furthermore, there might even be some doubt about whether these species are truly endangered, or even threatened, in any objective absolute sense. The bald eagle, northern spotted owl, Florida scrub jay, and grizzly bear, for example, have relatively large viable breeding populations that, while being pressed upon by habitat destruction in some places, do not appear to be even remotely exposed to any overall danger of going extinct. The same cannot be said, for example, of the Texas blind salamander, monitor gecko, Choctawahatchee beach mouse, or Waccamaw silverside, which are objectively much closer to extinction, but for any one of which total expenditures do not even come up to $10,000. . . . Only four are . . . species (bald eagle, West Indian manatee, whooping crane, red-cockaded woodpecker). The other six . . . are subspecies, [which] have very closely related near-twin subspecies, genetically almost identical, that are in virtually no danger of going extinct. At the opposite extreme are such creatures as the sand skink, red hills salamander, and Alabama cave fish. Total spending on any one is less than $10,000, yet each of these three endangered species forms a monotypic genus—meaning that they are the genetically distinct unique representative of an entire genus, having no sister species and being only very distantly related to their nearest safe cousin species in other genera.

The protection of a species entails a two-stage process: it is first listed officially as endangered, and then, once listed, the government decides how much money and effort to expend on its protection and recovery. The Metrick-Weitzman study shows that the listing decision conforms reasonably well to objective scientific criteria. In particular, a species is much more likely to be listed if it is more endangered as indicated by the ranking system of the Nature Conservancy and if it is a monotypic genus. Perhaps harder to understand is the preference accorded to mammals, birds, and reptiles, relative to fish, and, especially, to amphibians.

Most puzzling is the determination of the level of spending on a species once it has been listed. At this stage, the level of threat (represented by the Nature Conservancy ranking) and the degree of uniqueness (measured by whether the protected animal is a monotypic genus, a species, or a subspecies) play no significant role. The key matter appears to be whether the animal has charismatic qualities. This feature, rather than endangerment, seems to account for the membership of the top-ten spending list shown in table 10. Basically, people like bald eagles, and that is why they get so much attention.

Whatever the merits of preserving animals, the Endangered Species Act has to be viewed as a curious piece of legislation. On the one hand, the act pretends that unlimited costs should be borne to protect each endangered creature, including the taking of private property without compensation. On the other hand, the priority system implied by observed patterns of government spending suggests that cuteness counts a lot more than endangerment or uniqueness. Probably it would be better to start with a whole new approach, such as one that respects private property and provides a more rational basis for the allocation of scarce public funds.

Baseball Economics

In October 1994, the major league baseball players were on strike, and there was no World Series. In these circumstances, I found it difficult to sympathize with a person who was offered a million dollars to play baseball and nevertheless refused to work. But neither the players nor the owners in baseball or the other major sports are more greedy or honorable than the average person, and the serious issues concern the economics of the sports business.

On first appearance, the players seem to have the economics on their side. They argue mainly for free markets: that the owners not be allowed to disturb competitive bidding for players' services through caps or taxes on salaries or by other collusive devices. Normally, economists would find this argument compelling; after all, we like to rely on competition to generate efficient outcomes.

The sports business is, however, unusual in one key respect. To a considerable extent, a team's or athlete's output is measured not so much by absolute skill—how far a ball is hit or how fast a race is run—but by comparisons with the skills of other performers. How much difference would it make if the longest home run went 600 feet or 300 or whether 100 meters could be run in 8 or 10 seconds? These numbers matter mainly in relation to what other athletes can do (now and in the past).

The relative performance feature means that each team has too much incentive to hire the best athlete and that each athlete has too much incentive to raise his or her level of performance. Each time a team improves by hiring a better player, it effectively lowers the output of the competing teams. Each time a player gets more skillful, he or she effectively reduces the skill of the other players.

(The competitive interaction of sports teams differs from that among producers of ordinary goods, say, cars. If General Motors improves the quality of its cars, then Ford's revenues would likely suffer. But this kind of competition works through prices and revenues and does not cause any economic distortions. The effect of one sports team's actions on other teams is more like the situation in which a polluting firm damages the environment and does not have to pay compensation to those who are harmed.)

If competition among teams in a sports league is unrestricted, then the wages of players are bid up too high. The competitive wage for athletic skill reflects the benefit to an individual team of having a player who is better than the other players. In contrast, the "correct" wage from a social standpoint is the value of all teams' simultaneously having better players. Since the fans care a good deal about relative performance, the correct wage will be far below the competitive wage.

One consequence of the excessive wage is that players get more income and owners get less, a matter of great interest to the players and owners. The result is not only an income transfer, however, because the excessive wage causes a number of distortions. The main waste is that owners and players (and prospective players) use up too many resources in the process of improving skills. This activity is a social benefit only to the extent that fans care about the absolute level of talent. Another problem is that the number of teams tends to be too small. More teams could make profits and therefore survive if the players' wages were lower.

In one way or another, remedies for the wage problem must reduce the incentive of teams to compete for players. Baseball's reserve clause was especially effective until it was ruled unlawful. Other methods to suppress competition are a binding salary cap (or the less extreme arrangement of taxes levied on payments above designated levels), the new-player draft, and restrictions that require teams that sign a free agent to compensate the player's former team. One problem with these approaches is that they leave teams with an excessive incentive to compete; the schemes just block some of the obvious ways to bid for players. An even more ingenious scheme, used, for example, by the National Football League, prescribes a preset split of television revenues among the teams and thereby directly limits each team's return from winning. (This practice is, however, now being contested in various ways by Jerry Jones, the aggressive owner of the Dallas Cowboys football team.) The assignment of the best draft picks to the worst teams also helps to diminish the return from "success."

All of these devices can limit the waste of resources in the sports business, but they also imply large transfers of income from players to owners. Not surprisingly, the players' organizations in various sports have figured out this effect and have attempted to prevent or eliminate these schemes.

Players and owners often talk around the basic issue when they focus on competitive balance and the disadvantages of small-market teams. One suggestion is to tax the teams in large markets in order to subsidize those in small markets. This procedure does not address the basic problem of excessive wages because it does not reduce the incentive of teams to win by competing for players. In any event, if the owners find it desirable to subsidize small-market clubs, then they do not need the help of the players to implement this subsidy.

Although it seems like a different topic, the issue of drug use in sports is related to the questions just discussed. Suppose for the sake of argument that certain drugs enhance athletic performance but are adverse for health. An individual athlete has a great incentive to use the drugs because of the high return paid for superior results. But if all athletes use drugs and thereby raise the overall level of performance, then the fans benefit little because they do not care that much about the absolute level of skill. Since this benefit likely falls short of the health costs, everyone could be made better off by a collusive arrangement that prevented the use of drugs in sports. One approach is to enforce drug prohibition, but another is to lower the excessive wage paid for winning.

This argument should not be viewed as a general case for the prohibition of drugs. The logic would be different if drug use enhanced productivity in an area where the customers cared mainly about the absolute level of performance. Suppose, for example, that drug use improved the quality of singing. In this case, each singer would weigh the personal cost of drug use against the individual benefit in the form of higher wages for better singing. The outcomes would be correct from the stand-point of society (assuming that the audience cares about the quality of singing and not directly about drug use) because the wage accurately measures the value of an increase in singing quality. Thus, this reasoning would not rationalize the prohibition of drugs in most areas.

The main point is that calls for unrestricted competition among sports teams miss a key element of interaction among the teams. A better approach in this unusual business is to seek reasonable forms of collusive arrangements, in particular, ones that can contain excessive wages and curtail drug use. A likely possibility is that the professional sports leagues once had the balance between competition and collusion roughly correct but that the players' quest for higher wages has upset the equilibrium. On the bright side, however, the new world of bargaining in the sports business has raised the consulting income of economists.

Term Limits

To economists, term limits sound like minimum wages, rent controls, and similar interferences with free markets. In each case, the government tries to prevent a mutually advantageous trade: an employer hiring a low-productivity, hence low-wage, worker who is willing to work at that wage; a renter inducing an increase in the supply of housing by willingly paying a higher price; and an electorate choosing a desired representative who is willing to serve. The real surprise is that some strong supporters of free markets, such as the editorial page of the *Wall Street Journal* and congressional Republicans, have been the strongest advocates of term limits. What is going on here?

One argument is that incumbent politicians have unfair advantages in elections because of their ready access to campaign funds, staff, mailing and travel privileges, media publicity, and so on. Hence, the electorate is apparently fooled systematically by public relations barrages into supporting incumbents even when they are inferior to their challengers. This argument is similar to the Galbraith-like view that big corporations with massive advertising budgets can consistently dupe their customers into buying inferior products. Supporters of free markets and the capitalistic system reject this message because they have faith in the self-interested consumer to discipline the companies that do not deliver the goods. Advocates of the democratic electoral process ought to have similar confidence in the public not to reelect the officeholders who are providing unsatisfactory constituent services.

Another argument is that a citizen Congress with its continuing flow of fresh faces into Washington would result in better government than that provided by representatives with lengthy tenure. The counter argument is that experience is an important characteristic for legislators. Each viewpoint has some validity, and presumably the best solution is to let the market decide—that is, to allow the electorate to determine the proper balance between freshness and experience. Most of us would not want the government to determine whether the familiar or new brand of toothpaste is preferable. Why is a political representative different in this respect?

Many commentators have bemoaned the high tendency for incumbents to be reelected, often mentioning a typical success rate in excess of 95 percent for congressional incumbents. The electorate's threat to vote out a badly performing representative is a key mechanism that induces officeholders to behave. If the electoral control process is working, so that officeholders conform with the interests of the majority of their constituents, then the electorate rewards their representatives with reelection. If the public voted against satisfactory performers just to install a new face, then officeholders would have less incentive to behave, and the system would work badly. Thus, the main inference from a 95 percent reelection rate is that the political process is working and that officeholders are conforming to the wishes of their constituents. If we ever see a 50 percent reelection rate, then there really would be reason to worry.

The threat not to reelect works only if the incumbent is interested in another term (for the current, or possibly another, office). Thus, a problem of term limits is that it creates more lame ducks, who are less responsive to the desires of the electorate. Much has been made of Alexander Hamilton's reflections on this point in essay 72 of *The Federalist Papers*: "One ill effect of the exclusion [from reelection] would be a diminution of the inducements to good behavior." Since Hamilton had many good ideas, including a stress on the importance of governments' not defaulting on their debts, we should pay attention to his thoughts about the tenure of office. But it is interesting that Hamilton was arguing only that term limits on the *chief executive* were ill advised: "Nothing appears more plausible at first sight, nor more ill-founded upon close inspection, than a scheme . . . of continuing the *chief magistrate* in office for a certain time, and then excluding him from it, either for a limited period or forever after. This exclusion, whether temporary or perpetual, would have nearly the same effects; and these effects would be for the most part rather pernicious than salutary [italics added]." Thus, Hamilton was not discussing term limits on the legislature and was actually making an argument against the executive term limits contained now in the twenty-second Amendment to the U.S. Constitution.

The only respectable argument in favor of term limits that I know of refers to the legislature and involves the interaction with the seniority system, broadly construed. Representatives accumulate more power as they become more senior, partly because of better committee assignments and more staff and partly because of increased familiarity with government officials and institutions and with outside interest groups. Some aspects of this power, such as greater experience with governmental programs, are desirable; others, such as the increased ability to extract funds from interest groups, are undesirable.

An increase in seniority is bad if the costs from each representative's enhanced ability to divert resources to personal ends exceed the benefits from greater experience. However, even if seniority is a net cost in the aggregate, each district may choose to reelect its own incumbent (and would, if possible, vote against the incumbents from other districts). The voters behave this way because the relative seniority of their representative translates into a larger share of governmental largesse.

When relative seniority matters, the voters are trapped in what is called a prisoners' dilemma game. (In the classic prisoners' dilemma, two prisoners are better off if neither confesses than if both confess, but each is best off if he or she confesses while the other does not. The equilibrium without cooperation is where both confess, whereas that with a binding commitment is where neither confesses.) Everyone would be better off if they could reach a binding agreement that precluded the reelection of incumbents, that is, if term limits were instituted.

As an example, a few years ago, the voters of Washington State rejected a proposal that would have limited the seniority of their congressional representatives relative to those of other states. Yet the same voters likely would have approved a proposal that limited the terms of all congressional representatives, not just those from Washington. In any event, a decision in 1995 by the U.S. Supreme Court prevents states and localities from imposing term limits on their own representatives. These limits can now be enacted only by an amendment to the U.S. Constitution.

Changes in the seniority system may be an alternative to term limits as a way to avoid the prisoners' dilemma. If a representative's power to favor his or her district were invariant with seniority, then voters would not have an excessive incentive to reelect incumbents. One may, in fact, argue that the seniority system violates the Constitution's prescriptions about representation in the Congress: for instance, "the Senate of the United States shall be composed of two Senators from each State . . . and each Senator shall have one vote" may mean that each senator, and hence, each state, is supposed to have equal power, a situation clearly violated by the seniority system. (There would, however, also be a violation unless all senators were equally competent, an outcome that would be a challenge to ensure.) The constitutional argument against seniority is, in any case, a nonstarter because the Constitution also says, "Each House may determine the Rules of its Proceedings." Presumably we are supposed to pay attention even to the foolish parts of the Constitution.

Another problem is that the weakening of the seniority system in Congress would lose some of the genuine benefits of this system. Greater experience may justify positions of more authority, and, moreover, the rewards from seniority give Congress an efficient method to motivate good behavior from junior members. These arguments parallel the benefits from worker seniority in firms (or the usefulness of a parole system as a carrot to help control inmates in prisons). The formal system of seniority is also only part of the story; for example, members' increasing familiarity with interest groups is a kind of seniority that would not be eliminated by changes in the rules for committee assignments, staffing, and so on. Thus, it is unrealistic as well as undesirable to remove completely the operation of a seniority system in any legislature.

The various complexities about legislative term limits and their interaction with seniority do not arise for executive term limits. No prisoners' dilemma game applies, and the electorate can properly weigh experience, fresh ideas, the value of rewarding satisfactory performance in office, and so on. The only defense for executive term limits is that the electorate needs to be protected against itself, an argument that, if true, would mean that democracy was seriously flawed and would work much less well than it seems to. Thus, Hamilton was surely correct in *Federalist* number 72 when he argued against executive term limits.

The irony is that, since the passage of the Twenty-second Amendment in 1951, the United States has a two-term limit on the presidency. Moreover, some other countries with presidential systems have term limits (such as one six-year term in Mexico), and twenty-nine of the fifty U.S. states had some kind of term limit on the governor in 1991. (No limits were removed, and seven new ones were introduced since 1960.)

The prevalence of executive term limits reflects either bad public policy or my weak understanding of political theory. But the origins of these limits may have more to do with the competition between legislative and executive branches than with a desire to improve public policy.

The pressure for the Twenty-second Amendment reflected Congress's desire to shift the balance of power away from the executive, notably the wishes of the Republican-dominated House and Senate to preclude another powerful Democratic president who looked like Franklin Roosevelt. I am, however, unable to explain why three-fourths of the state legislatures voted to ratify this amendment and therefore voted to deny the public their right to reelect a president of their choice. To some extent, the current pressures for legislative term limits reflect the reverse desire to shift power away from Congress. From the standpoint of balance of power, it would surely be preferable to repeal the Twenty-second Amendment.

We can examine data to see whether the states with term limits on the governor have performed better or worse than those without such limits. The answer, holding constant geographic region and the level of per capita income in 1960, is that states with term limits experienced slightly *below* average growth of per capita income from 1960 to 1990 but were also a little below average in the fraction of state product that went to state and local government expenditures. Not surprisingly, the main message is that executive term limits were not an important factor in the determination of how fast a state grew or how much of the state product was spent by government.

My conclusion—based more on theoretical reasoning than on empirical evidence—is that executive term limits are a bad idea, but one should not expect vastly better performance at the state or national level from the elimination of these restrictions.

Legislative term limits are less clear-cut, and it is possible to build a respectable case that favors such limits. But it is unrealistic to think that the enactment of these limits would lead to great improvements in the functioning of governments and, hence, in the performance of the economy. The Republicans in the U.S. Congress should look elsewhere to find productive areas of reform.

George Stigler and the Chicago School*

In 1982, the U.S. economy was in a recession. George Stigler was awarded the Nobel Prize for economics, and the Reagan administration eagerly invited this kindred spirit to meet the press at the White House. No doubt in a desire to establish his political independence, George lost no time in describing the economic downturn as a depression and then, as he wrote in *Memoirs of an Unregulated Economist*, he "was removed from the platform in a manner reminiscent of vaudeville days, which is surely appropriate in a theatrical town."

One would like to praise George for his candor, but it was outrageous to classify 1982, during which the unemployment rate peaked at 10.8 percent in the fall, with the early 1930s and its unemployment rates of around 25 percent. George was right, however, that the 1982 recession was pretty bad.

George's abbreviated news conference in 1982 reminds us that he, like most other great economists, had his main influence on economics and economic policy through research and writings, not as a governmental policy adviser or by direct communication with the public. (He was offered a position as foreign trade adviser to President Nixon but fortunately

* I wrote the original version of this essay for the *Wall Street Journal* shortly after George Stigler's death in December 1991.

declined it.) George took seriously John Maynard Keynes's famous dictum (from his *General Theory*) about the subtle influence of economists: "The ideas of economists . . . both when they are right and when they are wrong, are more powerful than is commonly understood. . . . Practical men, who believe themselves to be quite exempt from any intellectual influences, are usually the slaves of some defunct economist. Madmen in authority, who hear voices in the air, are distilling their frenzy from some academic scribbler of a few years back." In the main, George avoided positions in government and allowed his academic scribblings to have an impact on policies and on views about the role of the state in economic affairs. In accord with Keynes's thinking, I have no doubt that his influence on policy and practical men exceeded that of any economist whom I can think of who has spent much time in Washington.

George, along with Milton Friedman, was a principal architect of the Chicago school of economics. George pointed out in his memoirs how he was responsible for Milton's coming to Chicago: "In the spring of 1946 I received the offer of a professorship from the University of Chicago . . . I went to Chicago, met with the President . . . and I was vetoed! I was too empirical. . . . So the professorship was offered to Milton Friedman, and President Colwell and I had launched the new Chicago School." It was not until 1958 that Stigler returned (in a much more lucrative position as Walgreen Professor) to Chicago, where he had earlier done his graduate work with the theorist and social philosopher, Frank Knight.

A key tenet of the Chicago school is that free markets function well in most circumstances and, hence, that government intervention into the economy ought to be minimal. A second theme is that economic analysis has substantial explanatory power for empirical phenomena, not only in the narrow economic realm but also (as Gary Becker has particularly demonstrated) in a wide variety of social interactions.

George's most distinctive contributions to the Chicago school involved studies of the actual effects of government regulations, such as in the electric utility and financial industries. Although early on George stressed the evils of monopoly and the hypothetical benefits of antitrust measures, he later became convinced that bigness is not necessarily bad and that the consequences of regulation and antitrust enforcement usually depart from the intended effects. The government often ends up hindering competition and promoting inefficiency.

For George, these typically poor outcomes raised the puzzle of why the government would nevertheless often intervene. He argued that we should look at the relative political influence of the winners and losers to predict what the government would do, as opposed to what it should do. Thus, tariffs can arise if the protected producers constitute a concentrated, effective lobby. By a similar logic, governmental agencies may act as protectors of monopoly privileges for the concentrated interest groups they are supposed to regulate. This type of analysis features strong interactions between economics and political science and has had a major impact on the topics and methods considered by political scientists.

Stigler received the Nobel Prize for the research that he had done in the 1960s on the economics of information. He showed how the dispersion of prices in a market would depend on the costs of search, and he used the framework to explain the role of advertising, retail stores, and other familiar features of markets. He showed that the maintenance of monopoly pricing was rendered difficult by the costs of observing competitors' prices, and he demonstrated that the government's practice of open bidding meant that it would typically pay high prices. This work on information opened up research areas that are now important in industrial organization, labor economics, and macroeconomics.

Stigler's first and continuing area of research was the history of economic thought. He went beyond mere description of changing economic theories to analyses of how ideas actually influence the work of followers and critics. In some cases, he used data on citations—references to earlier works—to measure objectively the impact of research on subsequent professional practice. (Some economists like to use counts of citations to construct rankings of researchers. Not surprisingly, this practice is criticized by people who lack many citations.)

George Stigler had a remarkable career, and his ability to continue productive research up to age eighty was likely due to the great variety of his interests. He was also known as a great wit, even to the many victims of his barbs, and his engaging writing style contributed to his wide readership. Thus, it seems fitting to close this discussion with the last piece of his wit that I know about.

George was organizing a meeting of the libertarian group, the Mont Pelerin Society, for August 1992 in Vancouver. He invited me to present a paper but pointed out that the society could reimburse only the "most economical method of travel." Knowing that George would never fly coach, I accepted the invitation but said that I would "follow your instructions and rely on first-class travel." This weak attempt at humor was squashed by Stigler's reply: "Allow plenty of time in hitchhiking to Vancouver." I shall miss his wit and his economics in roughly equal measure.

A Nobel Prize for Bob Lucas

When I was on the faculty of the economics department of the University of Chicago, I had a sign in my office that said, "No smoking, except for Bob Lucas." It was worth enduring the smoke to talk to Bob, but not to any other economist-smoker. This action reveals my belief that his selection for a Nobel Prize in Economics is a great idea, one that has been regarded as an eventual sure thing by most economists for many years.

Bob Lucas's contributions to macroeconomics in the 1970s permanently changed the very center of the discipline. Moreover, his influence has been as great on critics, primarily Keynesians, as on supporters, who tend to represent market-clearing or equilibrium-style approaches.

In some key articles published from 1972 to 1975, Bob applied John Muth's insights on rational expectations to monetary theories of the business cycle. Previous analyses had relied on simplistic Phillips curve models in which increased inflation led mechanically to lower unemployment and higher output. But these theories assumed that workers and firms did not exploit available information and thereby would commit the same mistakes time after time. For instance, higher inflation was assumed to raise the willingness to work because workers were continually fooled into thinking that their real wage was higher than it was.

In Bob's theory, where expectations are formed rationally, people can be confused temporarily by monetary surprises. (Rational expectations are not the same as complete information or perfect foresight.) In particular, an unanticipated expansion of money and the general price level may temporarily fool workers into thinking that their real wage had risen and producers into believing that the relative price of their product had gone up. Through these channels, a monetary stimulus may cause a temporary boom, but one that must end soon after the errors in expectations are recognized.

In the older style theory, the permanent tradeoff between inflation and unemployment meant that monetary policy had a key role in fine-tuning the economy. The revised theory has dramatically different implications because the monetary authority has its main influence when it does something surprising. Thus, it is not enough to print more money when the economy is contracting and to print less when the economy is expanding. The expectations of this policy pretty much neutralize the real effects, a result that was demonstrated in 1975 in an article by Tom Sargent and Neil Wallace.

Unfortunately, the easiest way for the monetary authority to create surprises is to behave erratically, an approach that has effects that are real but harmful. Therefore, an important policy inference from Lucas's theory is that the central bank ought to relinquish the idea of fine-tuning and instead concentrate on long-run objectives such as price stability.

As an aside, Bob's first theoretical paper on rational expectations, "Expectations and the Neutrality of Money," appeared in 1972 in a specialized publication, *The Journal of Economic Theory*. He had submitted it to the American Economic Association's main journal, *The American Economic Review*, but it was rejected on the grounds of being too mathematical. In response, Bob expressed outrage and accused the editor of trying to run *Newsweek*. All of this was confirmed by the editor, who asked what I would have done in his position. I am proud to say that my reply was that I would have accepted the paper instantly.

The role of expectations is not limited to monetary policy but is crucial in many areas of economics, as Bob showed in his later research on investment, unemployment, taxation, public debt management, and asset pricing. In all of these situations, the appropriate evaluation of policy must take account of the way that expectations would be rationally formed; the older analyses, which failed to consider this expectational adjustment, are now described as failing the "Lucas critique."

In the case of the Phillips curve, the critique means that the monetary authority cannot decide to expand money and prices during recessions and just assume that inflationary expectations will be the same. Similarly, policies on taxation, transfers, and regulation will typically be anticipated and will therefore affect behavior. Such notions are, of course, commonplace in theories of corporate finance; no self-respecting finance economist ever would have thought that the government could change a policy that affects financial markets—say a tax on capital income—and then neglect the consequences for the rational pricing of assets.

Aside from criticizing older methods of evaluating macroeconomic policy, Lucas showed how to develop fully articulated models that encompassed the rational formation of expectations. These models are now used regularly by macroeconomists to assess alternative policies. Much of this research, dubbed "real business cycle theory," has downplayed monetary factors and has focused on forces such as shifting technologies, changing patterns of international trade, and the government's fiscal and regulatory interventions. This emphasis on real forces also appears in recent research on the determinants of long-term economic growth, another area to which Lucas made a major contribution.

Lucas likes to view his contributions not so much in terms of their implications for specific controversies in macroeconomics—the Phillips curve, the effectiveness of monetary policy, the validity of Keynesian models—but rather as part of an evolving methodology for the whole field of economics. He says (in his *Models of Business Cycles*): "Dynamic economic theory . . . has simply been reinvented in the last 40 years. It is now entirely routine to analyze economic decision-makers as operating through time in a complex, probabilistic environment. . . . What people refer to as the 'rational expectations revolution' in macroeconomics is mainly the manifestation, in one field of application, of a development that is affecting all fields of application. To try to understand and explain these events as though they were primarily a reaction to Keynes and Keynesianism is futile." Thus, for Lucas, a useful approach to macroeconomics involves the same economic modeling that would work in corporate and public finance, industrial organization, and so on.

I cannot resist concluding with an anecdote. In the late 1970s, soon after I left Chicago, I invited Bob to present a paper to a seminar on macroeconomics that I was running at the University of Rochester. He was supposed to arrive the previous day, but I got a call from him that night. He said that he had gone to O'Hare to catch his flight to Rochester, but he learned at the airport that the smoking section of the plane was filled up. Therefore, he went home. I tried to contain my anxiety while remembering all the people who were eagerly anticipating Bob's talk the next day. So I gently inquired whether he might be able to catch a plane in the morning. He said that he had already explored this possibility but that the only smoking seats available were in first class. I said that first class would be fine, and Bob came and gave a great seminar. Actually, I would have been happy to pay much more than the extra airfare. (It is fortunate with the abolition of smoking on planes that Bob is now a nonsmoker.)

Oh to Be in England

Prologue

Toward the end of my year's stay at the Bank of England in May 1995, I wrote a light piece for the *Financial Times* on a foreigner's impressions of England. It uses economics only to a minor extent, and a couple of reviewers thought that it would fit better in a volume of humorous essays. But I do not have enough other humorous essays to fill a book, and my eleven-year-old son supplied the title, so I include here a revised version of my English impressions.

The Essay

A year's visit in England provides many insights and enjoyments. I have learned many new words and phrases, including *bap, nick, hob, yob, fixture, tearaway, panda car, busking, zebra crossing, bubble and squeak, mind the gap*, and *take away the whip*. There is even a pub outside the Chelsea Football Club's stadium called the *Cross Eyed Newt*, which is not, so far as I know, run by the Democratic opposition in the U.S. House of Representatives.

I was surprised that the two most prominent sports figures appear to be renowned especially for nonsports performances. Eric Cantona, the striker for Manchester United's soccer team, seems to be most noted for his karate kick of an unruly opposition fan. Will Carling, the captain of the England rugby team, is famous for describing the league's administrators as "57 old farts," following which he was terminated (apparently by the chief old fart) but subsequently reappointed after many expressions of outrage by fans and teammates. (More recently, Mr. Carling became known as a special friend of Princess Diana.)

My stay in England unfortunately confirmed that a dollar could buy a lot more goods and services in the United States.

Among the few items that I found to be cheaper in England were maps, newspapers, antiques, antiquarian economics books, black currant juice, publicly subsidized museums, theater (quality adjusted), prestigious private schools (also quality adjusted), and cleaning persons.

The government plays a large role in the United Kingdom, absorbing 41 percent of the gross domestic product in 1994; in comparison, the figure for the United States is a mere 34 percent. A trip to a Social Services office in West London yielded an array of brochures that described forty-six different types of welfare programs that people could apply for. Given this massive governmental presence, I was surprised to hear the outraged reaction to a proposal to require drivers to carry licenses with photographs. Americans regard this restriction as reasonable, but Britishers treat it as an unwarranted intrusion on civil liberties.

In contrast, people in England tolerate the required annual fee of £84.50 for a license to operate a color television set in one's home (reduced by £1.25 if one is legally blind). For some reason, the BBC, the beneficiary of this levy, is not yet a favored target of privatization.

The United Kingdom leads the United States in some areas of deregulation, notably in telecommunications. Imagine my excitement when I learned that I had a choice in local telephone service between the ex-government monopoly, BT, and an entrepreneurial cable television company, Videotron. Although I began with the already installed BT service, I figured that the addition of cable telephone would not only provide superior performance but also offer an opportunity to write about the wonders of competition and private production.

Things did not work out exactly as I had expected. The BT service was fine, although I was assured that things were different before the privatization of the mid-1980s. In contrast, it turned out to be a nightmare to deal with the upstart alternative, especially in terms of installation and billing. Thus, my faith in privatization and competition was dented, but surely not destroyed. (Actually, the cable telephone and television worked fine once they were installed, except that the sports coverage included too much cricket and not enough American football. Cricket would be a perfect case for the beer commercial that combines two activities in incongruous fashion; in this case, it would be baseball and monkey-in-the-middle.)

In the political arena, the Conservative prime minister, John Major, seemed honest and amiable but not especially conservative; for example, he seemed much more interested in higher taxes than in smaller government. He also suffered from comparison with his Reagan-like predecessor, Margaret Thatcher, who had strong views about the proper role of government at home and abroad. It was impossible to miss the parallel between John Major and George Bush.

The parallel continued with the Labour leader, Tony Blair, who resembled the Bill Clinton of 1992. In each case, an energetic "new Democrat" appealed to the political center and was more attractive than the lackluster incumbent. But Mr. Clinton in power showed little resemblance to a new Democrat, partly because he was pushed by left-wingers in his own party. The same thing would likely happen to Mr. Blair as prime minister. He would have to deal with party members like union leader Arthur Scargill, who remain opposed to relinquishing the Labour party's key socialist plank, the commitment to public ownership of the means of production, as set out in the infamous clause four of the party's manifesto.

A major ongoing problem for the Conservatives is their disarray over European union. This issue caused several rebellious members of parliament to be temporarily suspended from party privilege (lose the party whip) and later inspired a nearly successful leadership challenge to Mr. Major. The dissension seems odd because European union amounts to the creation of a larger, more centralized government, and one would have expected conservatives to have a clear negative opinion of this change. Probably the Conservatives in the United Kingdom in 1997 will suffer the fate of the Republicans in the United States in 1992 and will have to spend some years in the wilderness before being reborn and returned to power.

References

Alesina, A. and L. H. Summers (1992). Central Bank Independence and Macroeconomic Performance: Some Comparative Evidence. *Journal of Money, Credit and Banking* 25 (May): 151–162.

Aschauer, D. (1985). Fiscal Policy and Aggregate Demand. *American Economic Review* 75 (March): 117–127.

Aspe, P. (1993). *Economic Transformation the Mexican Way.* Cambridge MA: MIT Press.

Barro, R. J. (1984). Are Government Bonds Net Wealth? *Journal of Political Economy* 82 (November/December): 1095–1118.

Barro, R. J. (1996). Democracy and Growth. *Journal of Economic Growth* 1 (January).

Barro, R. J. and X. Sala-i-Martin (1991). Convergence across States and Regions. *Brookings Papers on Economic Activity* no. 1, 107–182.

Bollen, K. A. (1990). Political Democracy: Conceptual and Measurement Traps. *Studies in Comparative International Development* (spring): 7–24.

Buchanan, J. M. (1976). Barro on the Ricardian Equivalence Theorem. *Journal of Political Economy* 84 (April): 337–342.

Coleman, J. S. (1982). *High School Achievement: Public, Catholic, and Private Schools Compared.* New York: Basic Books.

Cutler, D. M. and L. F. Katz (1992). Rising Inequality? Changes in the Distribution of Income and Consumption in the 1980s. *American Economic Review* 82 (May): 546–551.

De Soto, H. (1989). *The Other Path: The Invisible Revolution in the Third World.* New York: Harper & Row.

Easterly, W. and S. Rebelo (1993). Fiscal Policy and Economic Growth: An Empirical Investigation. *Journal of Monetary Economics* 32 (December): 417–458.

Ecobichon, D. J. and J. M. Wu, eds. (1990). *Environmental Tobacco Smoke.* Lexington MA: Lexington Books.

Feenberg, D. and J. Poterba (1993). Income Inequality and the Incomes of Very High Income Taxpayers: Evidence from Tax Returns. In J. Poterba, ed., *Tax Policy and the Economy*, 7. Cambridge MA: MIT Press, 145–177.

Friedman, M. (1962). *Capitalism and Freedom.* Chicago: University of Chicago Press.

Friedman, M. and A. J. Schwartz (1963). *A Monetary History of the United States, 1867–1960.* Princeton NJ: Princeton University Press.

Gastil, R. D. and others (1982–83 and other years). *Freedom in the World.* Westport CT: Greenwood Press.

Hoxby, C. M. (1994). Do Private Schools Provide Competition for Public Schools? National Bureau of Economic Research, working paper no. 4978, December.

Keynes, J. M. (1935). *The General Theory of Employment, Interest, and Money.* London: Macmillan.

Knack, S. and P. Keefer (1994). Institutions and Economic Performance: Cross-Country Tests Using Alternative Institutional Measures. Unpublished paper. American University, February.

Lipset, S. M. (1959). Some Social Requisites of Democracy: Economic Development and Political Legitimacy. *American Political Science Review* 53: 69–105.

Lopez-de-Solanes, F., A. Shleifer, and R. Vishny (1995). Privatization in the United States. National Bureau of Economic Research, working paper no. 5113.

Lucas, R. E. (1972). Expectations and the Neutrality of Money. *Journal of Economic Theory* 4 (April): 103–124.

Lucas, R. E. (1987). *Models of Business Cycles.* Oxford: Basil Blackwell.

Metrick, A. and M. Weitzman (1995). Patterns of Behavior in Endangered Species Preservation. Unpublished paper, Harvard University, forthcoming in *Land Economics.*

Muth, J. (1961). Rational Expectations and the Theory of Price Movements. *Econometrica* 29 (July): 315–335.

Ricardo, D. (1817). *On the Principles of Political Economy and Taxation.* London: John Murray. Reprinted in P. Sraffa, ed., (1951). *Works of David Ricardo*, vol. 1. Cambridge: Cambridge University Press.

Ricardo, D. (1820). Funding System, an essay in the supplement to the *Encyclopedia Britannica.* Reprinted in P. Sraffa, ed., (1951). *Works of David Ricardo*, vol. 4, Cambridge: Cambridge University Press.

Sargent, T. J. and N. Wallace (1975). Rational Expectations, the Optimal Monetary Instrument, and the Optimal Money Supply Rule. *Journal of Political Economy* 83 (April): 241–254.

Stigler, G. J. (1988). *Memoirs of an Unregulated Economist.* New York: Basic Books.

Stroup, R. L. (1992). The Endangered Species Act: A Perverse Way to Protect Biodiversity. Bozeman MT: *Political Economy Research Center*, no. 11, April.

Young, A. (1992). A Tale of Two Cities: Factor Accumulation and Technical Change in Hong Kong and Singapore. In O. J. Blanchard and S. Fischer, eds., *NBER Macroeconomics Annual 1992.* Cambridge MA: MIT Press, 13–54.

Index

Jones, Jerry, 156
Journals, citation in, as rating
  of expertise, 85–89, 167
Journal of Economic Theory,
  169
*Journal of Monetary
  Economics*, 112
Journal of Political Economy,
  96

Kangaroo rat, 150
Katz, Lawrence, 116
Kennedy, President John F., 71,
  74
Kennedy School, Harvard
  University, 19
Keynes, John Maynard (and
  Keynesianism), 32, 84, 168,
  171
  General Theory, 165
Keynesian demand multiplier,
  110–111
Keyserling, Leon, 84
Knack, Stephen, and Philip
  Keefer, "Institutions and
  Economic Performance:
  Cross-Country Tests Using
  Alternative Institutional
  Measures," 4
Knight, Frank, 165
Kurds, 26, 31
Kuwait, 128

Labour party (U.K.), 18–19,
  174
Laffer curve, 39, 120, 126
Lame ducks, 159
Language, common, 31–31
Large countries, 30, 34–35
Libya, 128

Lincoln, Abraham, 27, 57
Lipset, Seymour Martin, 3
"Lipset hypothesis," 3
Lopez-de-Silanes, F., A. Shliefer,
  and R.Vishny, "Privatization
  in the United States,"
  138–142
Lower Saxony, 15
Lucas, Robert, 85, 168–171
  "Expectations and the
  Neutrality of Money," 169
  Models of Business Cycles,
  170
  "Lucas critique," 169

McCracken, Paul, 85
Macmillan, Prime Minister
  Harold, 81
Macroeconomic Annual, 24
Macroeconomic policy, a pro-
  gram for, 102–107
Maine, 13
Major, Prime Minister John,
  77, 80, 81, 174–175
Malawi, 10
Malaysia, 4
Mali, 10
Marcos, Ferdinand, 3
Massachusetts, 13, 32
Maturities, and indexed bonds,
  101–102
Mauritius, 10
Metrick, Andrew, and Martin
  Weitzman, "Patterns of
  Behavior in Endangered
  Species Preservation,"
  151–152
Mexico, 6, 10, 35, 40
  monetary policy in, 45–52
Migration, 15–16